D0972655

A Journey Through Emotional Abuse: From Bondage to Freedom

CAROLINE ABBOTT
with
DEBBIE STAFFORD,
Approved Domestic Violence
Treatment Provider, CAC III

A Journey
through
Emotional Abuse:
from Bondage to Freedom

CAROLINE ABBOTT
with
DEBBIE STAFFORD,
Approved Domestic Violence
Treatment Provider, CAC III

Published by
Carpenter's Son Publishing, Franklin, Tennessee
Published in association with
Larry Carpenter of Christian Book Services, LLC
www.christianbookservices.com
Printed in the United States of America
978-0-9885931-3-8
All rights reserved.

A Journey through Emotional Abuse: From Bondage to Freedom

©2013 by Caroline Abbott. All rights reserved. No part of this book may be reproduced or transmitted in any form or by any means, electronic or mechanical, including photocopying, recording or by any information storage and retrieval system, without permission in writing from the copyright owner.

Published by Carpenter's Son Publishing, Franklin, Tennessee. Published in association with Larry Carpenter of Christian Book Services, LLC www.christianbookservices.com

Unless otherwise noted, Scripture is taken from the HOLY BIBLE, NEW INTERNATIONAL VERSION®. Copyright © 1973, 1978, 1984 Biblica. Used by permission of Zondervan. All rights reserved. Cover and Interior Layout Design by Debbie Manning Sheppard. Editing by Virginia Bowen and Lorraine-Bossé Smith. Cover Image by Elena Elisseeva.

Printed in the United States of America. 978-0-9885931-3-8

DEDICATION

Dedicated to Christian women who are in difficult marriages, trying every day to make them better, yet they never seem to improve. My prayer is this book will shine light on the cause of your pain. May you come to understand God and the Bible do not condone your husband's treatment of you. Please know there is no guilt in seeking answers to the difficulties in your relationship. The Lord loves you with an infinite love, and wants to be your rescuer. God's love will carry you as you read this book.

Dedicated also to our children, and the children of our readers. May domestic violence not be passed down to another generation.

TABLE OF CONTENTS

TERMINOLOGY

This book is written primarily for Christian women who are being abused by their husbands. I acknowledge some men are abused by their wives, though that is not the majority. To make the book easier to read, and to maintain focus, I will refer to the abuser as "he" and the victim as "she." I refer to the abusive male in this book as the "husband." The same principles apply if you are not married to your abuser.

The term "pastor" is used for the leader of a church. Other churches call their leaders "minister," "priest," "father," or "rabbi" (in Messianic congregations).

Whenever names are used, they have been changed to protect the anonymity of victims of abuse.

The reader should understand "I" and "me" in this book refer to Caroline. However, Debbie lent her twenty years of experience as a domestic violence treatment provider to every page. The text in *Lifesavers from a Survivor* are from Caroline, and *Tips from an Expert* are from Debbie.

FOREWORD

If you find yourself waking up in the night feeling alone, afraid, in pain, or wondering if God is still there and if He is aware of what is happening to you, this book may help. Caroline first contacted me seeking an expert's view of domestic violence. Her story of suffering, denial, awareness, searching, and action have inspired me.

My story shows the sometimes subtle and sometimes blatant ways that verbal, psychological, emotional, and spiritual abuse can slowly erode one's mind, body, and soul. When I first had the courage to ask another pastor's wife, "What do you do if you are married and in pain?" she answered me by stating, "Once you are married, you are married. You really can't do anything." I went home feeling hopeless and alone. I want you to know you are not alone.

If you are hurting, God will be there for you and your family. As a pastor's wife, I had to face my shame and be honest with myself about what was really happening. One of the ways abusers continue their abuse is by isolating their victims. When I feared for my life and the lives of my children, I finally told my sister the truth and asked for help. God used her to help me, by bringing strong people to support me through my crisis. If you are ready to ask for help, this book is designed to give you the tools you need. John 8:32 says, "Then you will know the truth, and the truth will set you free."

May God carry you from your journey of pain to your journey of healing and freedom!

DEBBIE STAFFORD

ACKNOWLEDGEMENTS

I took several years to write this book. I began it as a way to heal from the abuse I had suffered during my own marriage. I had put it aside to be finished "one day," when the Lord woke me in the night and told me to finish it. Over the years, I had the opportunity to work with five different editors who helped me shape the vision for this book. Thank you to Candy Hein, Heidi Hess Saxton, Carolyn Goss, Virginia Bowen, and Lorraine Bossé-Smith. Without you great women, this book would never have been completed.

Thank you to Debbie Stafford, who brought her twenty years of experience in the field of domestic violence, as well as her own personal experience as the abused wife of a pastor, to the project.

Thank you to the women who helped me on my journey to understanding abuse. These include Christian friends, domestic violence advocates at the National Domestic Violence Hotline, and at my local women's crisis center. And to Patricia Evans, who wrote *The Verbally Abusive Relationship: How to Recognize it and How to Respond*. Without you, I would probably still be suffering under the bondage of abuse every day.

Thank you to my second husband, who was my greatest cheerleader. Whenever I got discouraged, he encouraged me by asking, "Whose idea was it for you to write this book? (God's) Then who will bring it to fruition?"

Most especially, thank you, Lord, for bringing it to fruition.

INTRODUCTION

My husband once told me, "Don't worry, I'll always be here to protect you from anyone who might hurt you." I remember thinking, "Who is going to protect me from *you*?"

Perhaps you've experienced such a startling moment of clarity and are admitting for the first time you are in a difficult—or even abusive—marriage. Or maybe you know someone you suspect is being abused.

You may not be able to identify the problem or explain the reason for it. You may be confused about what is happening to you and wonder why. Or you imagine if you ignore it, the whole thing will go away.

When I was in this situation, I could not find resources written especially for Christian women. Books I did find about marital abuse did not take into account my desire to follow the Lord and keep my marriage intact. The more I read, the more confused I became about how to handle the problem I faced.

> *My husband once told me, "I'll always be here to protect you."*
>
> *I remember thinking, Who will protect me from **you**?*
>
> *Perhaps that thought rings a bell with you or with someone you know . . .*

As a Christian woman, I knew the Bible verses about submission (Ephesians 5:22–24, Colossians 3:18, 1 Peter 3:1–6). But these only made my experience more difficult because, as I understood them, the verses did not permit me to resist my husband's behavior.

When I finally overcame my fear and told some Christian friends what was happening, things got worse. They counseled me to be as submissive as possible and stay in the marriage. But my friends did not understand an important truth about domestic violence: the abuse generally gets worse over time if the abuser is not confronted.[1] My submission empowered my husband to increase his abuse, making my marriage even more dangerous for my children and me.

So, if the Scriptures pertaining to submission didn't offer me any hope, are no other passages relevant in a domestic abuse situation? Yes there are—and you need to know about them—for yourself, or for the woman you know who needs hope.

I pray the Lord will minister to you as you read this book. May the Lord bless you, may He keep you, may He make His face shine upon you, and give you peace.

Caroline Abbott

SECTION 1:

Understanding the Whats and Whys of Abuse

CHAPTER 1:

What Is "Abuse"?

I felt I could not file for divorce to escape my husband's abusive behavior because of my faith. I was surrounded by people who counseled me to submit to my abusive husband, to "turn the other cheek," to "forgive and forget," and that "God hates divorce." This counsel compounded my pain. The implication was if I were a better wife, he would become a better husband. Unfortunately, few Christians—including pastors—have studied what the Bible says about abuse in marriage.

The first step is to identify what is meant by "abuse." *Merriam Webster's 11th Collegiate Dictionary* gives a definition that serves as a starting point:

> **Abuse:** a corrupt practice or custom, improper or excessive use or treatment; language that condemns or vilifies usually unjustly, intemperately, and angrily ("scathing verbal abuse"); physical maltreatment; misuse ("abuse of prescription drugs").

Next let's look at two types of relational abuse:

Physical Abuse

Some examples of physical abuse include:[2]

- Pushing, slapping, punching, biting, kicking, or strangling
- Throwing or otherwise destroying valued objects
- Harming children or pets
- Hair pulling
- Restraining or trapping
- Forcing you to leave your home
- Using a weapon to threaten or hurt you
- Driving recklessly
- Abandoning you in a dangerous or unfamiliar place
- Preventing you from calling police or seeking medical attention
- Using physical force in sexual situations

If you are in a marriage where your husband has been doing any of these things, *please,* put down this book and call the National Domestic Violence Hotline: 1-800-799-SAFE (7233) or 1-800-787-3224 (TTY) for further information. If you feel you, your children, or your pets are in immediate danger, call 911.[3]

Discovering you are in an abusive relationship is upsetting. You may react in different ways, and this is OK. You may become frightened and want to ignore the situation. Or, you may become angry and want to confront your husband with this new knowledge. I would caution you not to talk to him about this. An abuser's main purpose is to maintain power and control over his victim. You will be in much greater danger if he thinks he is losing control over you.

Emotional Abuse

Emotional abuse is more difficult to recognize because the victim does not have physical markings of the abuse. And, like all abuse, it is done in secret. Usually, only the recipient of the abuse (and possibly her children) ever hears it. To everyone else, her husband may be the greatest guy in the world! He may behave lovingly toward her when they are in public. He might be an elder at church, or even be the pastor of the church. He may be the life of the party, and the guy everyone calls when they need something—the one they would call when their car breaks down and they are stuck on the side of the road. Because of this, if she ever mentions what is happening at home, people may look at her like she is crazy.

In addition, it is confusing because the abuse becomes more intense over time. A woman would not begin a relationship with a man who called her names on the first date. The beginning of the relationship is always wonderful. Then it deteriorates slowly over time. Therefore, his partner becomes accustomed to his abuse, and she adapts to it.

Lifesaver from a Survivor

If you suspect you are being emotionally abused, educate yourself.

Then you can decide if you are a victim.

Finally, the behavior is justified or rationalized. The abuser blames his wife for his actions. He is wily and manipulative. He disguises his abuse to make her think she is responsible for his actions, or he is saying the things he does for her own good. He also denies or discounts her perception of the abuse, so that she begins to wonder if it is really happening or if she is imagining it.

Here is a list to help you decide whether you are being emotionally abused, which is summarized from Patricia Evans's book *The Verbally Abusive Relationship.*[4] You may not be experiencing all of these behaviors, but even if you are experiencing one or two, you likely are being emotionally abused:

1. He seems critical, hostile, irritated, or angry with you several times a week, although you hadn't meant to upset him. You are surprised each time. He may say he is not mad when you ask him what he's mad about, has "no idea what you are talking about," or tells you that it is your fault.

2. You never know what will set him off; he is unpredictable. One minute he is loving and tender, the next he is sullen, explosive, or angry.

3. He is jealous. He wants to know whom you have talked to and where you have been every minute of the day.

4. He is controlling. He might control all the money in the family, or tell you and the children what you are allowed to do or say.

5. He is self-centered. He rarely thinks about you or your feelings, but wants you to focus on his needs and feelings all the time.

6. He rarely, if ever, shares his thoughts or plans with you.

7. You are upset not so much about concrete issues—how much time to spend with each other or where to go on vacation—as about the communication in the relationship—what he thinks you said and what you heard him say.

8. When you feel hurt and try to discuss your upset feelings with him, you don't feel like the issue has been resolved, you don't feel happy and relieved, nor do you feel like you've "kissed and made up." He may say, "You're just trying to start an argument!" or in some other way express his refusal to discuss the situation.

9. You sometimes wonder if he perceives you as a separate person, because he doesn't accept your feelings or views as valid. He seems to take the opposite view from you on everything you mention, and his view is not qualified by "I think" or "I believe" or "I feel." It is as if your viewpoint is always wrong and his is always right.

10. You sometimes wonder, "What's wrong with me, I shouldn't feel so bad."

11. You can't recall saying to him, "Cut it out!" or "Stop it!"

His behavior leaves you feeling like you might be "going crazy." In fact, in their book *Stop! You're Driving Me Crazy,* George R. Bach and Ronald M. Deutsch call this "crazy-making" behavior.[5] If this is happening to you, you may feel that:

- You are always thrown off balance. You may be confused, and never be able to get a handle on the problem, though you might spend hours a day trying to figure it out. Your husband may constantly be breaking promises he makes to you and you are often surprised, even though you feel you should expect it.

- Because of his behavior, you may have "redundant, spinning circles of thoughts." You may feel disconnected, confused, and disoriented. You may feel lost, wandering around, not knowing where to turn for help. You may wonder if something is wrong, but not be able to put your finger on what it is, or feel that your world has become chaotic, and you cannot make sense of it.

- He may give you double messages. One day he will say "yes" about a subject, and the next day "no." When you ask him about it, he will deny ever having the first conversation, calling you crazy, or pretending to be concerned about your mental health. You find you stop asking for clarification about things he has said or promised. You might assume he wants the best for you, but he seems like he is trying to hurt you. You find you often experience the shattering of important dreams.

- You walk around with an uneasy, weird feeling of emptiness, or feel generally "bugged" whenever he is around. You feel pushed around and not in control of your own direction. Sometimes you have a strong wish to get away, yet you feel frozen and unable to move. All of this is hard to explain and hard to understand, but you know something is wrong.

- You begin to lose your self-confidence and start to doubt yourself. You lose your spontaneity and enthusiasm for life, and feel you must always be on guard. You develop an internal "critical voice," and are reluctant to accept your own perceptions because they always seem to be wrong.

- You start to feel uncertain about how other people read you, and you distrust your relationships ("Does she *really* like me, or is she stroking me?"). You start to believe the things you actually do best may be the things you do the worst.

Crazy-making behavior makes you feel:

- Thrown off balance
- Confused, disconnected, disoriented
- Experiencing spinning circles of redundant thoughts
- Having trouble putting your finger on what is wrong
- Increasingly out of control of your chaotic world
- Convinced your perceptions are wrong
- Distrustful of friendships
- As if you must live for the future and not the present

Do any of these descriptions sound like you?

- You have a tendency to live in the future ("Everything will be great when . . ."). You feel time is passing you by, and you are missing something. You wonder why you aren't happier. After all, you are married to a "nice guy" whom everyone loves.

Does this sound like your relationship with your husband? If so, most likely you are being emotionally abused.

The terms "emotional abuse" and "psychological abuse" are often used interchangeably with "verbal abuse." When these terms are set apart, verbal abuse most often refers to name-calling or yelling. Emotional abuse refers to the abuser putting his victim down, making her feel bad about herself, and saying things meant to wound her emotionally. Psychological abuse (also sometimes called "gaslighting"[6]), refers to the abuser's attempts to make the victim doubt her perception of events, her memory, and her sanity; i.e., making her think she is going crazy.[7] For the purposes of this book, and for simplicity's sake, I will use "emotional abuse" to refer to all of these.

Abusers will use other non-physical methods to keep control over their victims. My husband used all of these in addition to emotional abuse:

ECONOMIC ABUSE—keeping the victim from getting or keeping a job, making her ask for money, giving her an allowance, or taking her money.

SPIRITUAL ABUSE—twisting or distorting biblical Scripture to inflict guilt, or to gain control over his victim.

SEXUAL ABUSE—forcing her to do sexual acts against her will, or physically attacking the sexual parts of her body, or withholding sex from her. This can also include "reproductive coercion," where the abuser forces a woman to become pregnant against her will (perhaps by hiding her birth control or refusing to use a condom), or he forces her to have an abortion, or he kills her fetus.

CHAPTER 2:

What Is the Cycle of Abuse?

One of the reasons emotional abuse is so hard to identify is that it goes in cycles. At times, an abuser will behave in ways similar to those I described in Chapter 1. This is called the *explosive* stage.[8] But after that, he might behave wonderfully, much like he did when you first met. He will buy you flowers, take you on special dates, tell you how much he loves you, and that no one could love you as much as he does.

When he does this, you feel so wonderful! You say to yourself, "Oh, thank goodness! *This* is the man I married! He was just under a lot of stress last week," or "Maybe I imagined him saying those awful things," or "He is so sorry and has promised to do better, I know he won't act like that again."

Unfortunately, this is not the end of the abuse. This is just a stage of the abuse cycle. It is called the *honeymoon* or *hearts and flowers* stage. Your husband behaves this way to keep you from leaving him. No one wants to live with someone who is abusive all the time. If he behaves lovingly for a while, he knows you will want to forgive him and try to forget the way he has behaved before.

He acts this way for another reason. During the honeymoon stage, you let your guard down. You begin to trust him again, and you tell him things you would only tell a loved one. For example, you might share with him how you feel insecure with your new, younger leader at Bible study. While he has you in the honeymoon stage, he will comfort you and pretend to build up your confidence. In reality, he is storing up this information to be used to hurt you later on. The next time he is in the explosive stage, he will bring up your private conversations with him, but this time, he won't be comforting you. Instead, he might ridicule you and tell you what a wimp you are. "Who would want you in their Bible study group anyway? You can't even stand up to a twenty-five-year-old kid! You might as well quit that Bible study and stay at home with the children every day." This is perhaps what he has wanted you to do all along. If you are at home every day, you are much more isolated. You have less contact with friends and less of a support system if and when his abuse becomes more severe in the future.

You will also find yourself asking an abused woman's inevitable question when the explosive stage begins once more:

Why does he seem to love me sometimes and hate me at other times?

In my marriage, the honeymoon stage was wonderful, and I occasionally *did* forget some of the awful things he had said to me. This "forgetting" made it difficult for me to be honest with myself about what was really happening.

So I began to use the best tool I could think of to combat forgetfulness: I kept a journal. My journals helped me see exactly what was happening over time. I also found them very useful when, later, I needed to describe the abuse I had been suffering to my church, my friends, my family, and the courts. Remember, most abuse is seen only by the partner. Many times, the abuser is very well liked and respected in his business, in the church, and by his friends.

Lifesaver from a **Survivor**

Journal your experiences. The records will help you see what has happened over time, and help you describe the abuse if you need to later.

Make sure not to leave your journal where your spouse can read it.

One caution: do not leave your journals where your husband can find and read them. Mine did. He read them, and he told me how "crazy" I was. I am so thankful he did not destroy them. Keep your journals in a safe place, such as a safety deposit box or with a friend.

The honeymoon stage may last a few hours, weeks, months, or years. This is usually followed by a buildup of tension, where the partner feels like she is walking on eggshells. This part of the cycle is called the *tension building* stage. In this stage, a wife will do anything she can not to upset her husband. She will tell him anything she thinks he wants to hear, or withhold any information, feelings, or thoughts she thinks might set him off again.

Thinking of the abuser's behaviors as the repetitive, round-and-round cycle of abuse diagrammed by the Bridges Domestic and Sexual Violence Support Group can be helpful.[9] They describe the three emotions that keep the cycle going: love, hope, and fear:

- You **love** your partner, and the relationship has its good points.

- You **hope** the behavior will change because the relationship did not start out like this.

- You **fear** your partner will follow through with threats he has made against you or your loved ones.

Be aware some abusive relationships don't follow the honeymoon-tension building-explosion pattern. Some do not have a honeymoon stage. These abusers move from the explosive stage directly into the next tension building stage. Other abusers are so unpredictable they will sometimes skip the tension building stage and move from the honeymoon stage right into the next explosion.

A man can abuse his partner many ways. See the endnotes[10] for a list of websites describing types of emotional abuse in greater detail.

CHAPTER 3:

Does He Realize What He Is Doing?

Why would a husband, especially one who claims to know Christ, be emotionally abusive? I spent many hours/days/weeks/years asking myself this question. I spent years trying to explain to him how he made me feel. I thought if I could just explain it, he would understand what he was doing and would want to change. But whenever I tried to explain myself to him, he would invalidate my feelings. He became very adept at this. He would tell me:

1. What I remembered had never happened.
2. I was crazy.
3. I was picking a fight.
4. His behavior was my fault; if I would just stop provoking him, everything would be fine.
5. I wasn't "submitting to" or "respecting" him.
6. I didn't understand men.
7. I didn't understand the Bible.

I used to spend hours every day wondering whether my husband purposely behaved abusively, or if he was unable to control his behavior. Maybe you are asking yourself the same question. In his book *Why Does He DO That? Inside the Minds of Angry and Controlling Men,* Lundy Bancroft asks the same question. Then he answers it better than any other author I've found.

Lundy says he wrote the book so women would spend *less* time wondering *why* their abuser is doing what he is doing. When we spend so much time wondering why, we put the abuser at the center of our life, giving him more power to control us. Thinking about him, trying to fix ourselves for him, trying to make everything right for *him* becomes the all-consuming focus of our lives. In reality, who is supposed to be at the center of our lives?

Deuteronomy 6:5 says,

"Love the LORD your God with all your heart
and with all your soul and with all your strength."

So, given we are to focus our hearts and minds on the Lord, let us look at why an abuser behaves the way he does. Here are some common myths:[11]

1. He can't control himself.
2. He doesn't know how to handle his feelings.
3. He was abused as a child, and this is the only way he knows how to behave.
4. He is abusive because he faces so much discrimination outside of the home (either at work, or in society).
5. He has poor communication skills.
6. He hates women.
7. He has low self-esteem.
8. He's mentally ill.
9. He is addicted to drugs and/or alcohol.

Did you know…

Most men who abuse only their intimate partners and children have complete control over their behavior.

The reality may surprise you. While drugs and alcohol may make abuse worse, it is never the cause of the abuse. Most men who abuse only their intimate partners and children have complete control over when and why they behave abusively. They rarely lose control of themselves in other social situations. In general, they are able to keep control of their temper at their jobs and with their friends. They often have wonderful relationships with other women. They would rarely consider being abusive to their mothers. In fact, for the majority of abusers, the only time he behaves abusively is at home.

Why is that? In his mind, he abuses you because:

- He likes being in control.
- He has convinced himself that it is OK to act this way toward you.
- He gets what he wants by his behavior.

Let's look at a scenario of an abusive man getting what he wants by his abusive behavior. In this family, the father was supposed to do the dinner dishes on Wednesday nights. One Wednesday after dinner, he got up from the table and began watching television. His son said, "Dad, it's your turn to do the dishes." The father stood up and yelled at the top of his voice, "You little piece of crap! Who are you to tell me what to do? Who made the money that bought that food? Your b____ of a mother must have taught you to be so disrespectful to me! I'm not doing anything but sit here and watch my favorite program!" He finished by picking up a plate and throwing it against the wall. The mother and son quickly cleaned up the broken glass and scurried around to clean up the kitchen as quickly as they could. When dinner is finished the next Wednesday evening, no one says anything about Dad doing any dishes. He just goes and sits in front of the TV while his wife and son do the dishes without him.

> *"I'm entitled..."*
>
> *In reality, what he's saying is this:*
>
> *"I have special status in this family no one else has and it gives me certain rights."*

The main predictor for whether a man will be abusive is that he has a great feeling of entitlement.[12] *Entitlement* means he feels he has special status no one else in the family has. In his mind, he has the right to:

- Physical caretaking
- Emotional caretaking
- Sexual caretaking
- Deference ("Everyone should respect me, but I owe no one else any respect")
- Freedom from accountability ("No one should question my actions")

In contrast, the abuser's wife and children have very few, if any, rights.

Often, an abuser will try to hide the fact that he believes he is entitled to all of these things. For example, a husband might scream at his wife if she doesn't make a "decent" dinner each night, implying she is a "terrible mother." In reality, he probably doesn't care at all what the children eat—he feels *he* is entitled to a hot meal in front of him each night. Or, he may become enraged if she is talking to her mother on the phone when he comes home from work, saying they "can't afford" the phone bill. However, he may talk to his brother for an hour later that same evening.

What is really behind his anger? He feels she owes him her full attention when he comes home from work; she *owes* him special caretaking.

Your husband's feelings of entitlement mean you are not allowed to ask him about his behavior; in other words, he is free from accountability. If you dare to question him, he will become angry, blame his actions on you, act hurt, pretend the abuse never occurred, or say you are going crazy. Regardless, he will not take ownership of the abuse and make meaningful, lasting changes in his behavior.

CHAPTER 4:

Are Your Reactions Making the Situation Worse?

This is a good question to ask yourself. We can easily think, "My husband's actions are so wrong; I cannot be blamed for my bad reaction." Clearly, your husband abusing you is wrong. However, as a Christian woman, you will want to ask the Lord to reveal anything you might be doing or not doing that contributes to his wrong behavior. If you have done everything in your power to treat him with respect, and if you did not purposely provoke him, then *his anger is his problem.*

In Psalm 139:23–24, David searched his own heart:

Search me, O God, and know my heart;

test me and know my anxious thoughts.

See if there is any offensive way in me,

and lead me in the way everlasting.

During the last five years of my marriage, my mentor, Mary, encouraged me to search my heart to make sure I was responding to my husband in a way that honored the Lord. She gave me a small booklet called *Your Reactions Are Showing* by J. Allan Petersen,[13] which I summarize below.

Most Christians are pretty good at acting properly. The Bible gives many descriptions of how to behave (see the Ten Commandments in Exodus 20:1–17). But we probably don't realize our wrong *reactions* can hurt us as much as our wrong actions.

If you were to watch my actions, you wouldn't really know me. My actions don't reveal who I really am because they may be planned and rehearsed for your benefit. But my spontaneous, unconscious reactions *do* reveal who I really am.

Let me give you an example of how our reactions show our true nature. A baby is sitting in his playpen, playing happily with his toys. To us, he seems like a happy, content baby. But, if you put another baby in the playpen with him, watch out! As soon as Baby #2 grabs the toy from the first baby's hand, Baby #1 lets out a scream of resentment. Selfishness comes to the surface, and the reaction reveals what is *really* in the child's heart. The baby's reaction has demonstrated his true self.

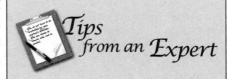

Tips from an Expert

You do not have to be controlled by your partner's behavior.

You can choose to remain calm and in control.

Here is an object lesson that also demonstrates this. Look at a tea bag. On the outside it looks white and pure. However, if you plunge it into hot water, what happens? Dark brown color flows from the bag and fills the entire cup. Let me ask you this: *Did the hot water fundamentally change what was inside the tea bag, or did it just bring out what was already there?*

What happens when you are plunged into hot water by your husband? Does something dark, brown, and unchristian flow out of you? Can you blame him for the brown liquid, or was this something that was in you to begin with? Let's see what Jesus said about this in Mark 7:20-23:

"What comes out of a man is what makes him 'unclean.'

For from within, out of men's hearts, come evil thoughts, sexual

immorality, theft, murder, adultery, greed, malice, deceit,

lewdness, envy, slander, arrogance and folly.

All these evils come from inside and make a man 'unclean.'"

My next question is this:

Who controls you?

Here is an example: If my husband tells me my housekeeping is terrible and I am a terrible wife and mother, and I respond that he is a slouch at work and a terrible husband and father, what have I done? I have responded to his unloving criticism of me with unloving criticism of my own.

He is now controlling me.

In this example, I would be controlled by my abusive husband and not by the Lord. As a Christian woman, I should not be under the control of anyone but Jesus Christ. Also, since an abuser's underlying purpose for abuse is to control me, I have played into his hands.

The question then becomes, "Can you do anything about your husband's actions? Can you *make* him treat you with love and respect? Can you make him stop cursing at you, withholding affection from you, or trying to control you?"

In reality, you cannot do *anything* about your husband's actions. The only person whose actions or reactions you can control are your own.

Realizing this is upsetting, but it actually empowers you. Though you have no control over your husband, and that is very frustrating, realize that, with the help of the Lord, you *do* have power over one thing: your behavior!

So, what should your reactions be? The Bible says that Christians should repay evil with good:

> *Lifesaver from a Survivor*
>
> You do not have the power to do **anything** about your husband's abusive actions. But you do have power over one person's behavior: yours.
>
> *Realizing you are not powerless can give you strength.*

> *Do not repay evil with evil or insult with insult,*
>
> *but with blessing, because to this you were called*
>
> *so that you may inherit a blessing.*
>
> *For, "Whoever would love life and see good days must keep*
>
> *his tongue from evil, and his lips from deceitful speech."*

(1 Peter 3:9–10)

I believe abuse in marriage is one of the things God would consider evil. However, we must know the importance of not adding to the problem by becoming abusive ourselves. The apostle Paul writes:

*If it is possible, **as far as it depends on you,***

live at peace with everyone.

(Romans 12:18, emphasis mine)

So, given you are living in an abusive marriage, how can you continue to do good?

1. Admit to the Lord what you have seen in your own heart.
2. Refuse to excuse any sinful behavior you've uncovered there.
3. Ask Him to help you change your thought patterns and behavior day by day.

The good news is this: you don't need to try to make these changes through your own power; you can use Christ's power to do it. As Jesus promises:

"I am the vine; you are the branches. If a man remains in me and I

in him, he will bear much fruit; apart from me you can do nothing. If

anyone does not remain in me, he is like a branch that is thrown away

and withers; such branches are picked up, thrown into the fire and

burned. If you remain in me and my words remain in you, ask whatever

you wish, and it will be given you. This is to my Father's glory, that you

bear much fruit, showing yourselves to be my disciples."

(John 15:5-8)

1 Peter 1:6-7 further explains the rewards in suffering:

In this you greatly rejoice, though now for a little while you may have

had to suffer grief in all kinds of trials. These have come so that your

faith—of greater worth than gold, which perishes even though refined

by fire—may be proved genuine and may result in praise, glory

and honor when Jesus Christ is revealed.

Isn't it wonderful the way you react to your situation may prove your faith is genuine, and will result in praise and honor for Jesus?

May I suggest you keep a journal of your experiences with your abuser? A journal is a personal document. You need not be concerned with grammar, spelling, or punctuation. Just record your honest thoughts, and put your journal in a place where only you—not your spouse, your parents, your children, or your friends—can find it. You can use any kind of paper or write in any notebook you like, or you can journal on your computer. (Perhaps a separate flash drive would work to store your journals.) Use this record as a way of communicating with God. Be sure to add dates, and don't be afraid to include both sorrows and joys. This journal can be a private communication between God and you, and He will write His truths to you in your heart.

A Drink of Water
for the **Journey**

Because of the LORD's great love we are not consumed, for his compassions never fail. They are new every morning; great is your faithfulness.

(Lamentations 3:22–23)

1. Have you experienced the three stages of abuse?

2. If so, did you find yourself trying to forget what had happened during the explosive stage when the honeymoon stage occurred?

3. Have you believed any of the myths about why an abuser behaves the way he does? If so, which one(s)?

4. What do you think about the idea that our reactions demonstrate who we *really* are?

5. Write a prayer to the Lord asking Him to search your heart. Then ask Him to help you react to your husband in ways that bring honor to Jesus.

SECTION 2:

Confronting Biblical Questions and Finding Answers

CHAPTER 5:

What Does the Bible Say About Submission in Marriage?

An abusive husband will often try to twist God's beautiful design for marriage by saying domestic violence is acceptable in light of God's call on women to submit to their husbands. Is this assertion true?

To answer this question, we must first note submission is *not* the same thing as obedience. Obedience comes from the word *obey*, which is defined by Merriam Webster's 11th Collegiate Dictionary as:

OBEY: to follow the commands or guidance of; to conform to or comply with (as in "obey an order").

Whereas submission comes from the word *submit* which is defined as:

SUBMIT: to yield oneself to the authority or will of another; to defer to or consent; to abide by the opinion or authority of another.

As we see from these definitions, a person obeys because they have no choice, they are being ordered to conform, as a child obeys a parent, or a marine obeys his sergeant. However, submission implies a woman *chooses* to yield herself to the will of another person; she consents out of her free will. A Christian woman, therefore, would choose to defer her will to her husband's out of love for him and out of love for and trust in the Lord Jesus Christ.

Let's look at what the apostle Paul says about Christian submission. Ephesians 5 is often used to describe submission only for women. However, it really describes submission for all people. This section begins in verse 21 with this directive:

*Submit to **one another** out of reverence for Christ.*

(emphasis mine)

It continues with additional instruction:

Wives, submit yourselves to your husbands as to the Lord. For the husband is the head of the wife as Christ is the head of the church, his body, of which he is the Savior. Now as the church submits to Christ, so also wives should submit to their husbands in everything.

An abuser might focus on the above three verses, but fail to apply the next seven verses to himself. Note as you read this passage that it is calling for *mutual* submission:

*Husbands, love your wives, just as Christ loved the church and **gave himself up for her** to make her holy, cleansing her by the washing with water through the word, and to present her to himself as a radiant church, without stain or wrinkle or any other blemish, but holy and blameless. In this same way, husbands ought to love their wives as their own bodies. He who loves his wife loves himself. After all, no one ever hated his own body, but **he feeds and cares for it,** just as Christ does the church—for we are members of his body. "For this reason a man will leave his father and mother and be united to his wife, and the two will become one flesh." This is a profound mystery—but I am talking about Christ and the church.*

(emphasis mine)

A husband who follows these seven verses is submitting his life and will to the Lord, but also to his wife. If he gives himself up for her, and cares for her as he does his own body, he is submitting his needs to hers. The apostle Paul sums up his discussion of Christian submission in marriage by saying:

However, each one of you also must love his wife as he loves

himself, and the wife must respect her husband.

John Piper, a renowned preacher, says headship in marriage does not give the husband the right to command and control his wife.[14] The husband has the responsibility of loving like Christ: to lay down his life for his wife's in servant leadership. And the submission of the wife is not slavish, coerced, or cowering. That's not the way Christ wants the church to respond to His leadership: He wants it to be free, willing, glad, refining, and strengthening.

In other words, Ephesians 5 does two things: it guards against the abuses of headship by telling husbands to love like Jesus; and it guards against the debasing of submission by telling wives to respond the way the church does to Christ.

Another set of verses that have been used to describe submission in the Bible come from Genesis 2:18–23:

The LORD God said, "It is not good for the man to be alone. I will make a helper suitable for him."

Now the LORD God had formed out of the ground all the beasts of the field and all the birds of the air. He brought them to the man to see what he would name them; and whatever the man called each living creature, that was its name.

In the Bible, the term **suitable helper** *does not connote a weaker, inferior, or subordinate position.* **Suitable** *means someone who is* **equal to** *the other person. And* **helper** *comes from the Hebrew word meaning to* **rescue,** *or to* **save.** *Her role may be different, but she is not less valuable or less important.*

So the man gave names to all the livestock, the birds of the air

and all the beasts of the field. But for Adam no suitable helper

was found. So the LORD God caused the man to fall into a deep

sleep; and while he was sleeping, he took one of the man's ribs

and closed up the place with flesh. Then the LORD God

made a woman from the rib he had taken out of the man,

and he brought her to the man.

The man said, "This is now bone of my bones, and flesh of my

flesh; she shall be called 'woman,' for she was taken out of man."

Biblical scholar Dr. Walter C. Kaiser says the word translated in the NIV as *helper* (which is used in Genesis 2:18 and 2:20 to describe the woman) comes from the Hebrew word *ezer* meaning "to rescue, to save," and/or possibly the word *gezer*, meaning, "to be strong." Furthermore, the word translated as *suitable* in the NIV comes from the Hebrew word *kĕnegdÔ* which means "corresponding to him" or "equal to him." Therefore, Dr. Kaiser's translation of the woman's position in the marriage would be *"a strong rescuer who is equal to the man."*[15]

Therefore, "suitable helper" does not connote a weaker, inferior, or subordinate position. Her role may be different, but she is not less valuable, or less important. Her role can be compared to the role of Jesus in the Holy Trinity. When Jesus was in the Garden of Gethsemane, He asked His Father to take away the cup of suffering He was just about to bear. Matthew 26:39–44 in the NIV reads:

Going a little farther, he fell with his face to the ground and prayed,

"My Father, if it is possible, may this cup be taken from me. Yet not

as I will, but as you will." Then he returned to his disciples and found

them sleeping. "Could you men not keep watch with me for one

hour?" he asked Peter. "Watch and pray so that you will not fall into

temptation. The spirit is willing, but the body is weak." He went away

a second time and prayed, "My Father, if it is not possible for this cup

to be taken away unless I drink it, may your will be done." When he came back, he again found them sleeping, because their eyes were

heavy. So he left them and went away once more and prayed the third

time, saying the same thing.

Once Jesus had prayed and asked God three times, He submitted himself to the Father's will, as we see in verses 45 and 46:

Then he returned to the disciples and said to them,

"Are you still sleeping and resting? Look, the hour is near, and

the Son of Man is betrayed into the hands of sinners. Rise, let

us go! Here comes my betrayer!"

When Peter cut off the ear of one of the soldiers, Jesus chided him in verses 53 and 54, saying:

"Do you think I cannot call on my Father,

and he will at once put at my disposal

more than twelve legions of angels?

But how then would the Scriptures be fulfilled

that say it must happen in this way?"

This is a great example of submission. Jesus, coming from a position of power as God's Son, the creator of the earth, *chose* to submit His will to His Father's so the Scriptures would be fulfilled, and so you and I could be forever in right relationship to God. In the same way, in the context of a loving marriage, God calls women to submit their lives and wills to their husbands. God has given the husband the role of leader in the home. His wife's role is to help him carry out whatever he feels God is calling him to do. This does not mean she must blindly do whatever he says without discussion. They are a team, and the two working together will be better than either of them working alone. However, in cases where they have a disagreement, she should lovingly, kindly allow him to lead, and trust the Lord that God will use her submission for His purposes.

But how can an abused wife use this advice?

A husband who is not abusive will respond favorably to a woman who loves him, thinks about him, and gives herself up for him. On the other hand, a man who is abusive will "ask for"—really, demand—more and more obedience from his wife. This type of man will not be won over by this behavior, but he will feel entitled to this treatment and will see it as another way he can control her. Using Bible verses to control is called spiritual abuse.

I tried to lovingly submit to my husband during my marriage. Not knowing which type of man my husband was, I prayed for him with a humble spirit. I tried in every way to honor the Lord in my actions toward my husband. I tried to behave lovingly and respectfully toward him, and I stopped lashing out at him when he was abusive. Unfortunately, these changes made him angrier and more abusive toward me.

I believe he became more abusive because he realized he was no longer in control of me. Since gaining control is the primary objective of an abusive husband, when I took control of my reactions I actually made him angrier. However, I have met other women who have struggled in their marriages, and this gentle and quiet spirit turned the hearts of their husbands around, to the point where marriages that were in deep trouble were made whole and beautiful again. Cultivating such a spirit worked for Stormie Omartian, author of *The Power of a Praying Wife,* and also for my mentor, Mary.

Because of the hardness of my husband's heart, nothing I did during the last years of my marriage would have caused a change in him. However, if I hadn't learned I was responsible for my own actions, I would have lost many things besides my marriage. My relationship with the Lord would have been damaged, as well as my relationships with others I loved, because I would have given in to anger and bitterness in my own life. Praise the Lord I learned that lesson when I did!

CHAPTER 6:

Can't God Change This Situation Through Prayer?

God *does* change things through prayer. However . . . His answers may not be what you would hope for or expect. When my marriage started getting worse, I didn't pray for my husband at first. I felt asking God to change him was conceited, so for years I only asked God to make me a better wife, and never asked Him to deal with my husband's behaviors, which really were sinful. A friend of mine mentioned the book *The Power of a Praying Wife* by Stormie Omartian many times, but I was in too much distress to even go get it for myself. Finally, one day she just handed me the book. Praise God for good friends!

The main thing I learned from *The Power of a Praying Wife* is that I couldn't change my husband. However, if my husband would let Him, God could change him. First, however, I needed to give up my desire to control my husband, and surrender to the Lord my justifiable woundedness. Each time my husband stabbed me with another word, I had to choose to forgive him. I could not allow each new hurt to grow a root of bitterness in my heart, or I would not be able to pray for him. This is no easy task for someone who is being emotionally abused! I took to heart Stormie's recommendation that I ask the Lord to show me the sin in *my* heart, and to help me put aside the hurt and anger I was feeling. She also suggested I ask the Lord to fulfill me in the areas I had been looking to my husband to fill. Fulfilling me was not my husband's job; that is God's job.[16]

The Power of a Praying Wife has thirty chapters, purposely designed so you can pray for your husband one chapter each day for a month. Stormie suggests these prayer concerns and others to help focus your prayers for your husband:[17]

- His work
- His finances
- His fatherhood
- His mind
- His temptations
- His choices
- His integrity
- His attitude
- His emotions
- His repentance
- His obedience
- His faith
- His future

Given my marriage ended in divorce, one might think the Lord did not answer my prayers. He did, however, keep my spirit from becoming bitter and angry. So, whether or not your husband allows God to change him is not the only sign of God answering prayer. He is able to change anyone who will let Him. Even if your husband won't change, God can protect your heart and spirit and continue to change you into the woman He wants you to become.

Hebrews 12:14–15 encourages us to watch our own attitudes:

Make every effort to live in peace with all men and to be holy;

without holiness no one will see the Lord.

See to it that no one misses the grace of God

and that no bitter root grows up

to cause trouble and defile many.

CHAPTER 7:

Does God Care About Abused Women?

Remembering God's Unfailing Love

Being in an abusive relationship is very painful. No matter how long you have been suffering in your marriage, you may be wondering if God cares about you, or if He even notices what is happening to you. The author of Psalm 77 had similar feelings:

> *I cried out to God for help;*
> *I cried out to God to hear me.*

> *When I was in distress, I sought the Lord;*
> *at night I stretched out untiring hands,*
> *and my soul refused to be comforted.*

> *I remembered you, O God, and I groaned;*
> *I mused, and my spirit grew faint.*

> *You kept my eyes from closing;*
> *I was too troubled to speak.*

> *I thought about the former days,*
> *the years of long ago;*

> *I remembered my songs in the night.*
> *My heart mused and my spirit inquired:*

> *"Will the Lord reject forever?*
> *Will he never show his favor again?*

> *Has his unfailing love vanished forever?*

43

Has his promise failed for all time?

Has God forgotten to be merciful?
Has he in anger withheld his compassion?"
Selah

***Then** I thought, "To this I will appeal:*
the years of the right hand of the Most High."

I will remember the deeds of the LORD;
yes, I will remember your miracles of long ago.

I will meditate on all your works
and consider all your mighty deeds.

Your ways, O God, are holy.
What god is so great as our God?

(Psalm 77:1–13, emphasis mine)

My mentor Mary showed me this Psalm. She pointed out that, at times, we can feel as if God's unfailing love has vanished forever, and that He has forgotten to be merciful and compassionate. When we dwell on our troubles, we sometimes cannot sleep, and we often cannot be comforted. The Psalm turns completely around in verse 10: "**Then** I thought . . ." Suddenly, the psalmist has turned his mind from all his troubles and all the ways that God has not helped him, and he begins to recount the deeds of the Lord and all His miracles of long ago. The Psalm ends on a huge note of praise and hopefulness.

How God Cared for Me

- God's word became more alive for me. As I read them, verses I had read many times before suddenly became real and personal to me. I grew to love the Psalms. Many Psalms, like Psalm 77 above, feature David crying out to the Lord, saying in essence, "This isn't *fair,* Lord! How can you let this happen to me?" As I saw how David drew comfort from all he knew to be true about God, I was also comforted in my pain.

- God spoke to me through Christian music. My daughter gave me the Mercy Me *Undone* CD. I listened to "Here with Me"[18] over and over as I drove in my car. As I sang this song, I could *feel* the Lord's loving arms around me. I knew I was not alone, and that He was calling me His own.

- God gave me wonderful friends. Though I tried to keep a "smiling" face to the world, they saw past my fake smile into my heart. They knew when things were going badly at home just by looking at me. They wouldn't accept it when I said everything was "fine." They lent a sympathetic ear, as well as innumerable prayers on my behalf, for many years.

- God gave me strength to face each day as it came, with His help and with His love.

- He gave me the courage to finally stand up to the abuse.

- Though you may struggle to believe it now, God cares for you, too, and will walk with you along your journey.

Christ's Love Surpasses Knowledge

Did you know every Christian is the bride of Christ? This Christ is the same Jesus who left the incredible beauty, majesty, and power of Heaven to come down to earth as a tiny squalling infant in a smelly barn. Why did He do this? He did it because He loves you. In fact, Luke 12:7 tells you the hairs on your head are numbered by the Lord. No human can ever love you the way God loves you.

The apostle Paul prayed we would understand this love:

> *And I pray that you, being rooted and established in love, may have power, together with all the saints, to grasp how wide and long and high and deep is the love of Christ, and to know this love that surpasses knowledge—that you may be filled to the measure of all the fullness of God.*
>
> (Ephesians 3:17b –19)

Jesus Loves and Defends the Widows

I have a friend who is a widow. She told me about a plumber who was trying to charge her more than he should for work he did. She felt he was taking advantage of her because he knew she had no husband. She told me she thought about saying to him, "You'd better watch out, you don't know who my husband is!"

This is humorous, but it makes a point that applies to you, even though you are married. As an abused wife, you are living without the covering of a loving husband to protect you. In this sense you *are* a widow, and in this same sense, your children are orphans. But . . . you are loved and protected by the God of the universe. The Bible's promises resound with hope for you and your children. Consider these:

A father to the fatherless,

a defender of widows,

is God in his holy dwelling.

(Psalm 68:5)

The LORD watches

over the alien and sustains

the fatherless and the widow,

but he frustrates the ways

of the wicked.

(Psalm 146:9)

I pray these verses will comfort you. In fact, if you will commit to reading the Psalms regularly, I am confident you will find promises in many that will encourage you at this difficult time, as they did for me.

A Drink of Water for the Journey

Cast your cares on the LORD
and he will sustain you;
he will never let the righteous
fall. But you, O God, will bring
down the wicked into the pit of
corruption; bloodthirsty
and deceitful men
will not live out half their days.
But as for me, I trust in you.

(Psalm 55:22-23)

1. Does your husband ever say you have to submit to his harmful behavior because the Bible calls wives to submit to their husbands?

2. After reading Chapter 5, what do you believe about submission in marriage? About submission to an abusive husband?

3. Have you been praying about your marriage? Do you struggle with any attitudes that might prevent you from praying for your husband? If so, write a prayer to God asking Him to change your heart.

4. Do you ever feel as if God has forgotten about you, or doesn't care what is happening to you?

5. Have you felt His comfort? If so, in what way?

6. Are you angry with God? He won't be shocked or angry if you are. He is a big God. He is big enough to handle whatever emotions you have toward Him. He already knows your innermost thoughts anyway. Spend some time in prayer, or journaling your feelings toward Him. Tell Him exactly what you feel. Then, spend some time *listening* for His response.

SECTION 3:

Taking Action to Protect the Innocent

CHAPTER 8:

How Can You Protect Your Children from the Abuse?

The sad truth is that while you and your children are living with an abuser, you have no immediate way to protect them from him. You might ask, "What if my husband focuses his abuse only on me, or we try to argue when the children are gone from the house or asleep?" Children are amazingly perceptive. They know when tension exists between their parents. This will cause them fear even if they are not being abused themselves.

Children living in abusive homes face many dangers most

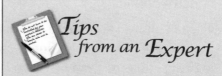

Tips from an Expert

Children tend to act out the pain of their parents. Some children may withdraw from the family, act younger than they are, or become the victims of bullies. Others become abusive themselves, usually picking on someone lower than themselves on the "pecking order." They may be aggressive toward their siblings, abusive to animals, or bully children in school.

people are not aware of. What follows may upset you, but this is important information every mother should know. Some of the following applies more to women in physically abusive homes, but as I have said earlier, if you do not make changes, your home may become physically abusive in the future. Be aware that all abuse, whether emotional or physical, will affect the children living in your home.

Here are some of the effects of raising a child in an abusive home:

- Children who experience childhood trauma, including witnessing or hearing incidents of domestic violence, are at a greater risk of having serious adult health problems, including tobacco use, alcoholism and substance abuse, heart and liver disease, sexually transmitted diseases, depression and suicide attempts, and are at a higher risk for unintended pregnancy.[19]

- Children from abusive homes have problems with attention and memory, impairment of visual-motor integration skills, lower IQ scores, and poorer language skills than children from non-abusive homes.[20]

- These children are five to seven times more likely to have significant psychological problems than other children.[21]

> *Did you know . . .*
>
> *More than 90 percent of prisoners experienced violence as a child. In fact, 63 percent of males aged eleven to twenty who commit murder kill their mother's abuser.*

- Often, children who live in abusive homes experience Post Traumatic Stress Disorder (PTSD).[22]

- More than 90 percent of prisoners experienced violence as a child.[23]

- Many children feel responsible for what is happening to their mother. Older sons may try to defend their mothers. In fact, 63 percent of males aged eleven to twenty who commit murder kill their mother's abuser.[24]

- Viewing abuse affects a child's ability to go to school, have healthy relationships, and be an employee.[25]

- Children tend to act out the pain of their parents. Some children may withdraw from the family. These children might act younger than they are, or become victims of bullies outside the home.[26]

- Other children will become abusive themselves. These children will usually pick on someone lower than themselves on the "pecking order." They may be aggressive toward their younger siblings, bully children in school, or abuse animals or household pets.[27]

- Some children may try to behave "perfectly," to prevent themselves and their mothers from being abused.[28]

- Others may act out, at home or at school, to get the worst possible punishment, so they can confirm to themselves that they are unworthy.[29]

- They may have survivor guilt. They may feel happy if they are not the one yelled at or beaten on a particular night, and then feel guilty about their happiness. They may think to themselves, "If only I had stepped in to protect my mom, or my sister, maybe they wouldn't have been so hurt. I'm such a terrible person."[30]

- Some children from abusive homes see school and work as an escape, and excel in these areas.[31]

- Others are afraid to leave their mothers to go to school. They become hyper-vigilant of her, never wanting to leave her side, thinking if they stay near her, they can prevent her from being harmed. They begin making up reasons for not going to school, finding imaginary (or not so imaginary) illnesses that will keep them at home so they can protect her. Soon, their schoolwork is affected.[32]

- While some children try to protect their mother, others, especially older children, identify with their fathers and lose respect for their mothers.[33]

- Some children are embarrassed by what is happening at home. Sadly, others come to assume abuse in the home is normal. They believe every home is like theirs. They assume even parents who appear loving in public become abusive when the doors are closed.[34] They grow up not realizing their childhood home was abusive.

By far, the worst outcome of raising children in an abusive home is the high likelihood they will become either an abuser or a victim of abuse in their future relationships. Men who, as children, witnessed their parents' domestic violence are **twice as likely to abuse their own partners** than sons of nonviolent parents.[35] However, in his talk entitled "Domestic Violence in Popular Culture" given at an Employers Against Domestic Violence event held at the Department of Revenue in Boston, Massachusetts on December 15, 2010,[36] Lundy Bancroft does shine a ray of hope for the sons of abused mothers. Mr. Bancroft cites recent studies showing when boys raised in abusive homes did not take on the attitudes of the abusers, they were not any more likely to abuse their partners in adulthood than boys who did not grow up in abusive homes.

The statistics above are frightening. Therefore, how should you raise your children in an abusive marriage? This is probably one of the most difficult questions you will have to ask yourself.

When I was in this situation, I was worried about the effect living with their abusive father would have on my children. But I confess I did not fully realize the extent of the long-term damage it might do. Knowing the pain of being raised in a divorced family, I was torn between my concern for the harm the abuse was causing, and the pain I knew they would endure if I divorced my husband. Also, I was convinced it would dishonor the Lord if I broke my wedding vows, so I was determined to make the marriage work.

Given my determination to stay in the marriage, I was concerned about the fact God calls us to honor our father and our mother in Exodus 20:12. At the same time, I didn't want my children to think the way their father was treating his family was the right thing for him to do.

My mentor Mary encouraged me to help the children respect their father's position in the home even if they could not always respect him for his behavior. She encouraged me to teach my children to respect my husband by setting a good example myself. She suggested I respond to him respectfully, especially when the children were watching. This way, the children had at least one parent modeling for them how God wanted them to behave. Our hope was that, as the children grew older, they would discern for themselves which of us behaved correctly (me), and follow my example.

This was my belief system at the time. Now when I look back, I realize how flawed it was. My mentor didn't fully comprehend I was being abused, and neither did I. Instead of being so concerned about teaching my children to respect their father, I should have set boundaries with my husband's abusive behavior (see Chapter 14), and showed my kids the way my husband treated me was *not* OK. Instead, I allowed them to see me being treated with disrespect, and this set them up to have erroneous beliefs about what a "Christian" marriage should look like. Because of my poor example, all my children have struggled with setting reasonable limits with people in their own lives.

Now that I have more insight into domestic violence, I realize my silence taught my children what we were experiencing as a family was OK. I had been taught that by my own family, and I was passing this lesson down to the next generation. I now understand that, to break this cycle of abuse, I would need to address my own denial and minimization of the emotional abuse my children and I experienced.

The journey of breaking the cycle of abuse in our family has been a long and painful one. When I finally recognized the severity of my circumstances and made the decision to leave, my children were older, and recognizing the long-term impact of the abuse on all of us was difficult.

A victim of abuse may become aware of the impact on her children before she realizes the impact on herself. Creating a safety plan for yourself and your children is very important. I'll go into the details of this plan in Chapter 10 "What is a Safety Plan, and Why is It Important?" but for this discussion, the truth to take to heart is this: your children have the right to feel safe in their own home, just as you do.

The time came in my marriage when my husband had been in an explosive stage for ten straight months. He had been giving me the silent treatment the entire time, except when he was raging at me. He started becoming physically violent:

- He pinned me to the floor with his body, so I couldn't escape during arguments.

- He told me he wanted me to die. After not speaking to me for weeks, one day, out of the blue, he said, "When you go out in your car today, I hope you get in a car accident and die." The next day, he calmly asked me, "How do you feel knowing I want you to die?"

- He woke me from a deep sleep early one morning. When I pulled the covers over my head, he yanked all the covers off the bed. I told him my heart was pounding. He said, "Good, maybe you'll have a heart attack and die."

- He hit me with the buckle of a belt. When I told him that hurt, he told me to "drop dead."

At the end of the ten months of the explosive stage, he insisted I tell our children he had never abused me. I knew I could not do this, for several reasons:

1. It was not true.

2. My children had seen the abuse, and I didn't want them to doubt their own perceptions of what had been happening.

> *Remember . . .*
>
> *Your children have a right to feel safe in their own home. You can make that your priority in various ways. Discuss those ways with them so they know what to do when they do not feel safe.*

3. If I told them their father had never abused me, I would have sent a message to them that what he had been doing was OK, and my daughters should not expect anything better from their husbands. In addition, my sons would get the message that treating their wives the same way would be OK.

After twenty years of marriage and almost five years of escalating abuse, this demand for me to lie was the impetus for me to *finally* permanently change not just my situation, but also that of my children.

Each marriage is different, and each woman needs to discern what the Lord is telling her. However, be aware our values and belief systems can affect how we understand the Bible. In John 8:32, Jesus says, "Then you will know the truth, and the truth will set you free." Once a mother begins to realize the effects of domestic violence on her children, she has a responsibility to consider how her choices are perpetuating the cycle of abuse in her children's lives, and in the lives of generations to come. In the next Chapter, I will tell you several ways to learn more about domestic violence.

CHAPTER 9:

Where Can You Turn for Information, Help, and Support?

Before I go further, I need to ask few things. Do you feel guilty for getting help for yourself? Do you feel disloyal to your husband when you read about emotional abuse? Does your husband accuse you of judging him if you tell someone what is happening in your home? If so, you are not alone. One of the ways an abusive husband can continue to abuse his wife is by making her feel guilty if she tries to tell anyone about it, or tries to get help in understanding what is happening to her. You are not being disloyal or selfish by getting some help. In fact, it may be the only thing that will save your marriage . . . and possibly your life.

Once you get past your worries about searching for help, you can turn to many people and places for information and support. Not all of them will have a "Christian" label on them, but that is OK. God can use unbelievers as well as believers to help you.

The Internet

The Internet can be very helpful, but be careful where and how you use it. Your husband can easily trace the websites you have viewed on your home computer. If you are concerned he might be monitoring your computer, you might want to use a computer in a friend's home or nearby library.

The National Domestic Violence Hotline has a very good website that can be accessed at **www.thehotline.org.** This website has a "quick escape" button you can push to immediately close the page. This is great, but the record of your visit can still be found if your husband is savvy enough to search for it.

You can reach another great site here: **www.troubledwith.com.** This *is* Christian, and it is run by Focus on the Family. This site has many helpful articles on subjects such as physical and emotional abuse, sexual abuse, and depression. I also invite you to visit my website at www.carolineab-bott.com, where I have many articles about domestic violence.

You can find a wealth of other articles on the Internet by searching for "emotional abuse" and "domestic violence."

Libraries and Bookstores

You can also find some outstanding books on abuse in the library or bookstore, or even on Amazon.com. See the Appendix for a list of books to read.

The National Domestic Violence Hotline

At one particularly desperate point in my marriage, I went to my phone book and looked up the National Domestic Violence Hotline, 1-800-799-SAFE (7233) or 1-800-787-3224 (TTY). I began telling my story to the woman who answered the phone. She was compassionate and knowledgeable. I don't know whether or not she was a Christian, and it didn't matter. What mattered was she was willing to listen to me for an entire hour, and she understood immediately the way my husband was behaving was emotional abuse, bordering on physical abuse. She was the first person to tell me point blank I was being abused, and I believed her.

This hotline is a great resource. *If your husband is likely to monitor your phone calls, use caution* when calling this or any other hotline.

Women's Crisis Centers

The woman at the National Domestic Violence Hotline gave me a phone number for my nearest women's crisis center. Although I was aware women's crisis centers existed, I always pictured the women who went there as physically beaten up by drunken, slovenly husbands. I never thought I would need their services! I was also unaware most of these centers provide counseling at a very minimal cost, or completely free if necessary. Although my husband was wealthy, he kept a very tight rein on my finances. I appreciated access to the counseling I needed. I was also unaware you don't need to live at the center to receive this help. They had counselors available, to anyone who needed them, at a different location.

Like the woman at the hotline, the counselor I visited was very compassionate and knowledgeable. I had been struggling greatly with whether God's will for me could possibly be to separate from my husband. One of my greatest fears was my Christian friends would look down on me if I did separate from him. My counselor helped me think through my fears about this.

Counselor: Do you think God wants you and your children to stay in a situation that is this dangerous and unhealthy?

Me: I'm not sure.

Counselor: What questions are you struggling with?

Me: I know it may sound funny, but I'm afraid what my Christian friends would think of me if I separated from my hus-

> Guilt says "I have done something wrong."
> Shame says, "I *am* something wrong."
> Many people allow their shame at being abused prevent them from getting the help they need.

band. I'm afraid all those people who think so highly of me right now will begin to look down on me, and maybe even shun me.

Counselor: Do you think those people who *really* know you, if they knew what was happening at home, would *want* you to stay there?

Me: Well, no, of course not...

Support Groups

The crisis center also offered support groups for abused women, and I joined one. I found many of the women to be very much like me, which surprised me. Other women had backgrounds very different from mine, but I was amazed how familiar their stories of abuse were. We began to recognize many patterns among abusers. I was relieved to be able to be completely honest with these women. They believed me and didn't question my motives or behavior; after all, they were experiencing the same things I was.

One woman, who I will call Ann, had been living with her emotionally abusive boyfriend for seventeen years. They had been running a business together for the last fifteen years. The company bore his name because he was somewhat famous in their field. However, she did all the marketing, all the phone calling, all the billing, and all the customer care, day in and day out.

I was startled by how similar our stories were:

Ann: Well, I was so tired last night after doing all the billing for the month. I just wanted to go home and climb into a warm bath and read a book. Jeff had been on a business trip for ten days, and I had really been enjoying the peace and quiet. Even though he rarely speaks to me anymore at home, I feel like I'm walking on eggshells whenever he is there. I had just sunk down into the warm water when the door slammed open, and he started screaming at me!

Me: Why was he screaming?

Ann: Apparently I should have read his mind, known he was coming home at that moment, and should have had dinner waiting on the table for him! He never even bothered to tell me when he was flying in! Before he left, he hadn't spoken a single word to me in nine days, and he didn't call me once while he was gone, so how was I supposed to know when he'd be home?

Me: I know what you mean, my husband sometimes goes for a month without speaking to me; then, out of the blue, he will start yelling about something I am supposedly doing to him "on purpose." I never know *when* he might explode next.

Counselors

Whenever I described my marriage to friends, they would usually tell me my husband and I needed to go to a counselor together. However, according to the US Department of Justice, "Many practitioners disapprove of—and at least twenty state standards and guidelines expressly prohibit—couples counseling for batterers."[37]

In her book *Battered but Not Broken: Help for Abused Wives and Their Church Families,* Patricia Riddle Gaddis also warns against couples counseling with an abuser. She says, "Unfortunately, despite the fact that the National Coalition Against Domestic Violence speaks out strongly against couples counseling, many professional counselors and pastors continue to engage in it."[38] Ms. Gaddis continues:

> *"Never attempt to counsel a couple together if violence is in the relationship.* Unless the abuse has totally stopped for many years, and the abuser has completed a program designed specifically for batterers, couples counseling will only serve to increase the risk of danger to the woman. This is because battering is a control issue and not a communication issue, and couples counseling poses a major threat to the abuser's control over the relationship. In order for couples counseling to be effective, equality is needed between the partners involved. Unfortunately, when the dark veil of violence hovers over a relationship, no equality exists in the communication process during the sessions because the woman will fear future retaliation for her honesty. This not only makes the marital counseling process ineffective; it also places her life at risk."[39]

Because of this risk, the better approach is to seek help on your own. After you have done some work to understand what is happening to you and how you can safely respond, you can get an expert's opinion whether couples counseling would be safe. Please consider this very carefully, since you do not want to be put in more danger than you already are. Your husband should do group counseling specifically for batterers, if he is willing to do this.

Lifesaver from a **Survivor**

Two tips about counseling:

1. Do **not** go with your husband if he is an abuser.

2. Make sure you go to a counselor who is an **expert** in domestic violence.

I discovered the most important thing about a counselor is that he or she is an expert in domestic violence. Not knowing that it is unwise to go to couples counseling with an abuser, I went with my husband to a very well-meaning Christian counselor for six months who was not trained specifically in domestic violence. It truly was a waste of my time, and it *did* make my husband's emotional abuse escalate. Although the counselor was very sympathetic to me, he would say things like, "We need to find out what happened in your past that makes your husband's behavior hurt you so much." In a year, I finally realized my husband's abuse would hurt *anyone,* and that, in fact, his behavior was *designed* to hurt me.

I found out later my local women's crisis center had a list of counselors who were trained in domestic violence, and that many of them work on a sliding fee scale (i.e. they charge what a client can afford). Another resource is Focus on the Family (1-800-AFAMILY), which has lists of Christian counselors all over the country.

Not until things were truly desperate did I finally get helpful counseling. I wish I had received counseling from an expert in domestic violence long before I did.

Mentors

When my husband's abuse first began to escalate, I went to my church office and asked for a list of wise, older, godly women who would be willing to mentor me. My church did have such a list. My mentor Mary walked me through the last five years of my marriage, which were extremely difficult.

When I first began meeting with her, I regularly reacted to my husband's abusive behavior with anger and disrespect. The first time we met, I told her about an incident that had happened the previous weekend:

Me: Last Friday, my husband got really angry with me because I overcooked his steak. He stopped talking to me for two days. By Sunday night, I couldn't stand it anymore. After the kids were in bed, I went up to where he was sitting in his favorite chair in front of the TV, and asked him why he wasn't talking to me. He called me a b____. I was *furious!* I told him he had no right to talk to me that way! He said calmly, "Well, you are a b____." I said, "That's a nice way for a Sunday school teacher to talk!" I picked up a nearby magazine and threw it at him! He just sat there and *smiled* at me! I said, "What is so funny? Do you enjoy seeing me like this?" Then he said quietly, "Oh, you are just so out of control." Then he went back to watching his TV show.

Mary: What did you do then?

Me: I ran upstairs to my room, and slammed the door so hard that a painting fell off the wall. Then I cried myself to sleep.

Mary: I can see why having him call you that name would have upset you, and I am sorry, but I'd like you to think about something.

Me: What's that?

Mary: I know he behaved badly, but didn't you end up behaving just as badly in the end?

Me: Well, yes . . .

Mary: As a follower of Jesus, we should strive not to be controlled by anyone else but Him. In that instance, you allowed your husband's behavior to control how you behaved. I wonder if you would consider reading a little book I have called *Your Reactions Are Showing?* I think it might help you respond to your husband's behavior in a more God-honoring way. Would you be willing to do that?

Me: Sure, I guess so . . .

Mary was a godly woman, but she was not schooled in dealing with abuse. I eventually had to seek additional advice when the abuse escalated, advice more specific to domestic violence. However, I am thankful she helped me keep my eyes on Jesus throughout the last several years.

Friends and Family

One of the best methods abusers use to continue their bad behavior is to isolate their victims. Abuse thrives in secret. Abusers will resort to all types of threats and mind games to prevent their victims from telling anyone what is happening at home. Their children are taught to keep this secret, as well. Therefore, one of the best ways to fight abuse is to reveal the secret to safe people you can trust, and get as much support from friends and family as you can. Many therapists say, "We are as sick as we are secret."

Lifesaver from a Survivor

Abuse thrives in secret.

Therefore, one of the best ways to fight abuse is to reveal the secret to safe people you trust. That way you're educating them, protecting yourself and your children, and enlisting their support.

This doesn't mean you should tell your story to every person you meet; it is good to use discretion. Wisely find friends and family members who will be supportive of you during this difficult time.

Not every friend and family member will be good support for you. Many will insist on telling you what to do, which is *not* what you need right now. After all, you already have a person at home telling you what to do, don't you? People who think they know what is best for you may fall into one of two camps:

- They will say you should stay in the marriage no matter what; or

- They will say you should *get out now!*

Because of this, you might need to coach your friends on some things that would help you right now:

1. Don't demand proof of the abuse. I may not have any proof you can see. Just believe me and be there for me.

2. Don't bad-mouth my husband. When you do that, I feel like I need to defend him.

3. Don't tell me what I "have to" do. I have enough of that at home. Helping me think through my options would be a lot more helpful.

4. If you give me an ultimatum, like "If you go back to him one more time, I wash my hands of you," then I won't be able to confide in you anymore.

My friends became my lifeline during the last years of my marriage. Many times, just telling a friend what was happening lightened my burden. Two of my friends gave me a key to their house so I could have a safe, quiet place to go to when things were really painful at home. I was able to go there and read my Bible, write in my journal, talk freely on the telephone, even sleep when my emotional distress left me exhausted. Their encouragement and prayers helped me carry on during a very difficult time. *Note: this was during a time when my husband was not threatening me or following me. I was confident I was not putting my friends in danger.*

Cultivating friendships may be difficult for some abused women, especially if their husbands are extremely controlling. If you have a husband who has limited the number of people you come in contact with, or who asks you many questions every time you are apart from him, this will be a challenge. See if you can talk to friends over the phone or meet them when he is at work.

I learned firsthand how valuable my friends were by their love for me when I was at my lowest point.

CHAPTER 10:

What Is a Safety Plan, and Why Is It Important?

The first day I went to our marriage counselor alone, I described some of the veiled threats my husband had been making. The first thing the counselor said was, "Do you have a safety plan?" I was shocked. I was in such denial that I didn't think I needed to do that.

I didn't follow his advice. Then, out of the blue, my husband ripped the covers off me one morning when I was still asleep, and told me he hoped I would die. I ran from the house wearing only my nightgown. Thank the Lord it was summer, or I would have frozen. I began getting items together that afternoon so that if I ever again needed to leave the house quickly, I could do it safely.

Does this mean you will have to leave your home at some time in the future? Not necessarily. But, as the Lord says in Proverbs 22:3:

> A prudent man sees danger and
> takes refuge, but the simple keep
> going and suffer for it.

In other words, better to be safe than sorry.

I recommend you call your local women's crisis center or the National Domestic Violence Hotline when making your safety plan. I include below the items in a standard safety plan.

Lifesaver from a Survivor

Having a safety plan for you, your children, and your pets is essential.

"A prudent man
sees danger and takes refuge,
but the simple keep going
and suffer for it."

Proverbs 22:3

Items to Have Packed and Ready to Go

If you have your own car and your husband is unlikely to snoop in it, you can store your things in it. I stored mine in my trunk in a Rubbermaid box with a lid, so he would not be likely to wonder what was inside and open it. If you are afraid he might find your things and get angry, ask someone you trust to hold your things for you. If they will give you a key to their house, or the code to open their garage, that's even better, in case you need to leave when they are not home.

Here is a list of the items you should have available:

- *An extra house key, work key, and car key.* (Note: some car manufacturers make duplicating the keys to their cars impossible and costly. This was true of my 2000 Toyota Land Cruiser. If I used a copy on my car, the engine would seize up, and the car would be inoperable. I couldn't believe this, but my local dealer confirmed it. I began wearing clothes with pockets and keeping my keys on my body at all times. At night, I slept with my purse next to my bed. Sometimes car dealers can order a spare set of keys for you at a reasonable cost.)

- *Cash, credit cards, checkbooks, account numbers, ATM cards.* If your credit cards and bank accounts are held jointly with your husband, cash is best for two reasons. The first is he can cancel any accounts he jointly owns. The second is he can trace your whereabouts by tracking where you use your cards or write checks. Be aware of any bills that come to your home, or accounts he can access via the Internet.

- *Address book, phone numbers, addresses, and directions to safe places.* A safe place could be the house of a friend (not someone on your block, in case your husband might see you), a women's crisis center, or even a motel where your husband would not expect you to go. Because you will probably be afraid when you need to go there, make sure you have directions.

- *At least one change of clothes for you and each of your children,* and coats, hats, gloves, etc. during cold weather.

If you are planning to leave for an extended period of time, you may want to remind yourself where the following items are so you can quickly grab them, or collect the ones you can set aside:

- Extra eyeglasses/contacts

- Medications

- Family pictures

- Jewelry

- Small, salable items (that you could pawn for cash)

- Your children's favorite toys or blankets

- Important papers, such as house and car deeds, mortgage payment book, rental agreements, birth certificates, passports, green cards, social security cards, driver's license and registration, insurance information, school and vaccination records, marriage license

- Bibles, journals, pictures, or anything else that might help you prove abuse

Cautionary Notes

- *Leave your cell phone behind.* Your husband could find you through your cell phone, since most have tracking devices now. Write down important phone numbers and keep them with you at all times.

- *Do not use your current email, Facebook, or Twitter account,* especially if you plan to post recent pictures you've taken with a digital camera. These cameras store a code of the date, time, and place they were taken.

Lifesaver from a Survivor

Your husband might try to track you by these methods:

- Bank accounts or credit card bills

- Your cell phone

- Your email or Facebook

- Small tracking devices he can place anywhere

- *Your husband might hide a very small tracking device* on other items such as the underside or inside of your car, the inside of your purse, or even inside your child's favorite teddy bear.

- One friend I know did an entire *household inventory with serial numbers, date purchased, value, and photos so that she had docu-*

mentation of what they had. This could be helpful later on when splitting assets with your husband. However, this might be too stressful when preparing a plan for your safety. Your main focus is to get you, your children, and your pets out of the abuse and to a safe place.

Call the National Domestic Violence Hotline: 1-800-799-SAFE (7233) or 1-800-787-3224 (TTY), or your nearest domestic violence crisis center to confirm your safety plan. They will have the latest information on methods to keep you and your children safe.

Special Populations

Leaving an abuser is difficult for every woman. Some women have special life circumstances that make leaving even more complicated. Some examples are:

- Immigrant women
- Women whose spouses are in the military
- Women living in rural areas
- Women with disabilities
- Elderly women
- Women of color
- And many others

If you are one of these women, leaving your abuser safely may seem a hopeless dream. However, talking to a domestic violence advocate to help you create your safety plan could save your life. You might need to enlist a friend to make the call. Ask the Lord to give you the strength and creativity to overcome the obstacles in front of you.

If You Must Leave in a Hurry

If you need to leave quickly but have not packed the above items, do not wait to get them. Your physical safety is your first concern. Leave the

Lifesaver from a Survivor

If you must leave quickly

Get your children and leave everything else behind.

Do not return to your home alone under any circumstances.

house as quickly as possible and get to a safe place. You can try to get back into your home later with a "civil assist" by a police officer. Do *not* return to your home alone to retrieve them, even if you think he would not be home at that time. I know of several women who went back alone, and were killed by their abusers.

Safety Planning for Your Children

Your children also have the right to feel safe. The best way to ensure their safety is to be safe yourself. However, some things can be done to protect them even while you are in an abusive situation. These actions will depend on your situation, their age, and maturity level:[40]

- Give them a pillow to hold when they are frightened. Tell them they can punch it or scream into it if they are feeling angry.

- Choose a "safe spot" together, somewhere in your home they can go when your husband becomes abusive, such as into a closet, or under their bed.

- Teach them how to call 911 and give them permission to do it if they are afraid for you or for themselves.

- Identify one or more nearby neighbors they can go to when they are afraid. Talk to these neighbors with your children so they know they have a safe adult they can tell about the abuse.

- Decide on a "code word" together. You can say this word to let them know they should leave the house or call the police.

Safety Planning for Your Pets

An abuser will often use threats against pets to control his victim; either to keep her from leaving, or to make her return against her will. Because of this, it is important to create a safety plan for your pets as well. Here are some items to have ready for your pets:

- Leash

- Food (and bowls)

- Pet carrier

- Medications

- Pet chewing toy or bone (Animals sense stress and will be under duress as well.)

If you must leave urgently, your first priority should be to get your children and yourself to safety, but take your pets if at all possible. Women's crisis centers have become aware of abusers' use of pets to control their victims. Some centers now take in the pets of victims.

CHAPTER 11:

What Should You Do if the Abuse Turns Physical?

He May Already Be Physically Abusive

Though you may not have bruises on your body, he may already be doing things many experts and law enforcement authorities consider physically abusive. Take a look at the following list. Ask yourself if he is:

- Making threats to physically hurt you, lunging toward you as if to physically hurt you.

- Scaring you by driving recklessly.

- Destroying objects you care about.

- Damaging property when angry (throwing objects, punching walls, kicking doors, ripping telephones out of the wall, and similar actions).

- Throwing things toward you (even if they don't hit you).

- Holding you so you cannot leave a room, trapping you in your home, or locking you out of your home.

- Abandoning you in a dangerous or unfamiliar place.

- Using a weapon to threaten you.

- Hurting children or pets.

- Using physical force in sexual situations.

- Preventing you from accessing a telephone to call the police.

- If he is doing any of these things, he is *already* physically abusive.

Prepare for the Worst

Of course, you have no way to predict whether an emotional abuser will become physically abusive. Your husband may remain emotionally abusive toward you for the rest of his life, and never become physically abusive. However, if not confronted, abuse tends to worsen over time.

Being prepared for the chance he may one day become physically violent toward you, your children, or your pets is wise.

If and when that day comes, most likely you will be caught off guard and in shock. You will not know how to react. That moment is not the best time to come up with a plan of action. Even though this may seem frightening to consider, be wise and think about some of the following questions before a situation occurs:

1. **What would be the best way to react so he will not continue hurting you at that moment?** What physical posture should you take to protect yourself? What (if anything) should you say?

2. **What would you do if your children witnessed him physically hurting you?** Would you rather remain quiet, or tell them to go somewhere safe?

> *You cannot predict whether your husband will become physically abusive. If he does, you may be shocked. Be wise, and come up with a plan **before** this happens.*

3. **Would you want to involve the police?** What if someone else calls the police, even if you don't want them to?

Getting the police involved may be very helpful, or it may not be, depending on how prepared you are to talk with them. The following is what to do if the police are called.

What Can You Expect If You or Someone Else Calls the Police?

Police response to domestic violence calls varies greatly, depending on the state and police district where you live. The best thing you can do is educate yourself. First, you can educate yourself by calling your local domestic violence hotline and asking them to describe what happens when police come to a domestic violence call in your area. Then, call the non-emergency line of your local police department and ask to speak to a domestic violence or victim's advocate. If they don't have one, ask to speak to an officer. Then, confirm the information given you by the domestic violence hotline. You may decide making one or both of these calls from a phone number that cannot be traced back to you is prudent.

Here is a list of the some questions you might want to ask:

1. How many officers usually answer a domestic violence call?

2. If they determine probable cause a crime has been committed, do they have a mandatory arrest policy in your area? In other words, are they instructed to arrest someone if they suspect domestic violence, even without anyone pressing charges?

3. Does your police department have a domestic violence advocate available twenty-four hours per day? When would they be called? Could you request they come to the scene?

4. Do the officers interview the man and woman in the same room, or do they interview them separately, giving the woman privacy to speak openly?

5. Do the officers generally investigate to determine which of you is the usual aggressor, or do they arrest whoever has the fewest wounds? In other words, do they try to figure out which person is controlling the other in the relationship? He may have more wounds on him if you were acting in self-defense.

6. If they can't determine who is at fault, how often do they arrest both the man and the woman? Do they often arrest the woman only? What would happen to the children in these cases?

7. If no one is arrested, would they give you time to pack some things, and would they be willing to take you to a safe place? Would you be able to take your children?

8. If your husband were arrested, what would happen next?

9. Would the court automatically issue a mandatory restraining order against him for you?

10. How much time would he spend in jail?

11. If charged, would he be forced to enroll in a domestic violence treatment program for offenders?

You may not think you need to look into this because you don't plan to ever call the police. However, a neighbor may call them one night if they hear arguing, so the police may suddenly end up on your doorstep. Your children, or even your husband, might call them. If your husband calls, you face the possibility that *you* might end up being arrested and taken to jail.

Below are four different scenarios of police responses you might expect.

Type 1: Old-Fashioned Response

One day your husband, who until that point has been emotionally but not physically abusive, picks up a marble paperweight off your coffee table and throws it at you, knocking you in the head. You pass out for a minute. When you wake up, he has gone into another room, so you grab the phone, which you take into your bedroom, locking the door behind you. You call 911.

Within minutes, two police officers arrive. Your husband meets them at the door and invites them in. He begins telling them how you had been nagging him all day, and he finally "lost it." He picked up the paperweight just to "show you who is boss," and you rushed at him, knocking your head into it.

Officer #1 under his breath to Officer #2: "Here we go again. Just like my first two wives. Worthless and stupid!"

Officer #2, to Officer #1: "Yeah, right—and mean. We need to teach these broads who's boss."

One of the officers turns to you. "Now, ma'am, you need to learn not to be such a nag. Get hold of yourself. Calm down."

Neither of the officers takes the time to investigate what happened. They leave the house after about fifteen minutes. Officer #1 tells you, "If you can't get along, just get a divorce, lady." Officer #2 says, "If we have to come back again tonight, we are going to throw you *both* in jail."

Without realizing it, these officers have just given your husband the green light to beat you. Your husband knows you won't call them again and risk both of you being arrested.

Type 2: First Uneducated Response in a Probable Cause, Mandatory Arrest State

Your husband has been emotionally abusive for years, but he has never once hit you. Lately, he has started drinking with "the boys" after work. You are sick of it. When he finally comes home after midnight one night, you start yelling at him. To your shock, he punches you in the face. As you fall to your knees in pain, watching blood pour from your mouth, your husband pins you to the floor and holds you there, laughing in your face. You tell him to let you go, over and over again. Finally, you start to panic. You reach up and scratch him in the face, leaving four long red marks down his left cheek. He lets go of your arms to grab his face, and you roll away from him and go hide in your bathroom.

Meanwhile, your teenage daughter, who recently had a class in high school about self-defense, decides to call the police. She has had enough of her dad treating you this way, too! Five minutes later, a knock is at the door, and you hear, "Police, open up!"

Now what?

Your daughter goes to answer the door, telling the officers what has happened. Your husband meets them in the hall, and shows them the scratch marks on his face, which are now swelling into ugly red welts. He tells them his "b---h" of a wife scratched him for no reason. You walk out of the bathroom, sure you are safe now, and show the officers your bloody mouth.

The officers are tired. This is their third domestic violence call that evening, and they still have several hours on their shift. They have not had much training in domestic violence, and the state has recently changed its laws, which now stipulate that if probable cause exists a crime has been committed in a domestic violence case, an arrest must be made. First they listen to your husband's story, then yours, then your daughter's. Then they listen to them all again. Things get more and more confusing. Finally, they tell you they can't figure out who started it, and they decide to arrest both of you.

Type 3: Second Uneducated Response in a Probable Cause, Mandatory Arrest State

Your husband has been emotionally abusive for years, and it has gotten much worse lately. You are beginning to be very afraid of him; in fact, you are thinking about leaving him. He realizes something is different about you, and he doesn't like it. He starts arguing with you at the dinner table one night, and you try to walk away from him.

Suddenly, he grabs your arm. You start screaming loudly and try to pull your arm away from him, but he pulls you toward him. The next thing you know, he has his arm around your neck! You panic and begin screaming, "Help!" He laughs, and says, "This is funny, I wonder why I never did this before?" You decide you had better do something quickly, so you open your mouth and bite down on his arm as hard as you can, leaving red teeth marks on his skin. He lets you go, and you run to your bedroom and lock yourself in.

Your husband is furious! He yells to no one in particular, "How dare that 'b---h' bite me? Who does she think she is? I'll show her!" He picks up his cell phone and calls 911. He tells them, "My 'crazy' wife became abusive, and bit me for no reason. Would you please come out and stop her before she really hurts me?"

The police arrive within ten minutes, and your husband greets them. He shows them the bite marks you left on his arm, and pretends to be a loving husband who is "afraid" of his wife. Back in your room, you hear the police arrive, and you come into the hall. The police ask to see any physical marks your husband has left on you, but bruises wouldn't show yet; you have no marks to show them.

The police ask you to tell your story, but they don't remove your husband from the room. You are afraid to talk to them with your husband right there! You think to yourself, "what if they don't arrest him? Who knows what will happen to me if I tell them what really happened. I'd better just keep my mouth shut."

So you tell them nothing. The older cop says, "Lady, you'd better speak up. We don't like to arrest broads, but he's the only one with any marks on him." The younger officer looks sympathetic and says, "I suspect you might be an abused woman, but if you don't speak up, we can't help you." Your mind keeps spinning in circles. You look over at your husband, who glares at you. You think about the hell he might put you through if you tell them he had been strangling you. Finally, the older cop says, "Well, lady, this state has a 'probable cause, mandatory arrest' policy regarding domestic violence. So, we have to arrest one of you. Since your husband has bite marks on his arm, and you look OK, we are going to have to arrest you. You have the right to remain silent . . ."

Type 4: Progressive, Educated Response

This is a similar situation to Type 3, just described. Your husband grabs you and begins to strangle you. Only, in this scenario, you live in an apartment. The woman next door, Nancy, is listening at the wall. Nancy has heard you arguing ever since she moved in five months ago, and you know she has been upset the entire time because she has asked you several times if you were OK. She grew up with an abusive father who finally killed her mother. Nancy has tried to talk to you several times, but you have always lied and told her everything was fine at home. She has told you that she has promised herself if she ever heard your husband doing anything physical to you, she would call the police. When she hears you scream "Help!" she picks up the phone and dials 911.

Not knowing the police are on the way, you bite your husband's arm. When he lets you go, you run to Nancy's apartment, where she quickly opens the door and lets you in. When the police arrive, your husband greets them. He shows them the bite marks on his arm, and pretends to be a timid husband who is "afraid" of his wife. You come over from Nancy's apartment. The police ask to see any physical marks your husband has left on you, but bruises wouldn't show yet; you have no marks to show them.

However, the police in this district have been trained in domestic violence. They recognize that a bite mark on a forearm is often a self-defense wound, inflicted when someone is being strangled. They ask if you would like a domestic violence advocate to be called. You say you would like that. She won't arrive for about thirty minutes. In the meantime, the two officers separate you and your husband. One officer takes your husband's statement in your kitchen, while the other officer tries to take your statement in Nancy's kitchen. You are afraid to talk to him, so he begins by taking Nancy's statement.

Thirty minutes later, the DV advocate arrives, and begins talking to you. First she asks you if you feel safe. You tell her no, you do not feel safe. You say you are afraid to tell the police what really happened because, if you do, your husband will be really angry. She explains to you that your state is a mandatory arrest state. You have never heard of that! You ask her what that means. She says if the police have probable cause to believe a crime was committed in a domestic violence case, someone will have to be arrested. The DV advocate also explains the district attorney will offer you a no contact order, so your husband will be barred from your home, and not allowed to contact you at all, or he will be arrested again. You think about it for a while, and decide having *him* arrested is better.

So, you give the officers your complete statement, which matches the statement of your neighbor, Nancy. While you are giving your statement, the younger officer examines your neck more closely. He notices a few slight scratches, which he takes pictures of. He also notices your voice sounds raspy, and he takes an audio recording of you talking. He asks you if that is the way your voice usually sounds. You are surprised, because you hadn't noticed anything different, but now that he mentions it, both you and Nancy agree your voice *does* sound a bit different. He hands you a glass of water, and remarks you seem to be having a hard time swallowing.

The officer calls an ambulance to come examine you. You protest, saying you feel fine. The DV advocate explains bruising from strangulation on the inside of the throat can cause death, sometimes as much as thirty-six hours later. You decide you *will* go with the EMTs.

The officers take all the evidence into consideration:

- Your husband's statement
- Your statement
- Your neighbor's statement
- The position of the bite mark on your husband's forearm
- The scratches on your neck
- Your raspy voice
- Your difficulty swallowing

They decide all the evidence supports your claim that your husband tried to strangle you, and you bit him in self-defense, and they decide to arrest him.

What happens in this scenario once someone is arrested?

In this progressive district, DV offenders are taken to jail and promised a hearing by a judge the next day. At that time, the defendant is offered three choices:

- He or she can plead guilty
- He or she can plead innocent and have a trial date set
- He or she can choose to meet with the district attorney, who will offer them a plea bargain

In the meantime, the victim is:

- Offered medical care if appropriate
- Contacted by a victim's advocate from the police department
- May be advised to relocate for safety, or moved to a battered women's crisis center if room is available
- If children were present and neglected, or suspected of being harmed, human services will be called

- If pets are involved, they may need to be relocated for safety

- A restraining order may be issued by the court

- The victim is not allowed to recant. In other words, he or she cannot tell the court nothing happened or ask that charges be dropped—once the defendant is in custody, the state presses charges, not the victim

What happens next?

If the defendant is found guilty, after jail time is served, or if he/she pleads guilty, he or she will be put on probation and assigned a probation officer, and usually will be ordered by the court to take domestic violence or anger management classes.

Does the Possibility Your Husband Might Become Physically Abusive Frighten You?

It should. Your life, the lives of your children, and your pets might suddenly be in danger. Because of this, it is important that you:

- Do not remain in denial—recognize if you aren't safe

- Create a safety plan for you, your children, and your pets

- Implement your safety plan if and when you feel that is necessary

- Realize you don't have the power to change your husband, but you do have the power to change yourself and your reactions

CHAPTER 12:

What Happens if Social Services Is Called?

Mandatory Reporting of Child Abuse

Be aware each state has a list of people legally mandated to report suspected or known child abuse. This includes:

- *Counselors*
- *Medical professionals*
- *Clergy*
- *Law enforcement*
- *Attorneys*
- *Teachers*
- *Crisis center workers, etc.*

Check your state's laws.

During one of my visits with a crisis center counselor, I mentioned my husband had hit our daughter a few weeks earlier, leaving red welts on her arm. I watched the blood drain from her face. She told me she was mandated by law to report this to social services. I was horrified. I had no idea when speaking to a counselor I might be getting involved with social services. Apparently, my private counselor and lawyer were also mandated to report this. Neither of them had followed through and actually reported it, however.

That day at the crisis center, I called my attorney to ask her advice. She said for me to not report this myself, as that would look vindictive toward my husband in a court hearing. Meanwhile, the counselor at the crisis center advised me to report it myself, because it would look better to social services. She advised me if I didn't report it, they might take the children away from me because I was not able to keep my children safe. I was truly between the proverbial rock and a hard place!

We finally compromised. The crisis center counselor called social services while I was in the room. She told them she was making the report because the mother (I) hadn't known this was required by law.

I was told social services was required to come and see the children within forty-eight hours of a report. When the social worker arrived at my house the next day, she came in and asked me a lot of questions. She then told me she would have to check all of my children for bruises. I turned pale. I knew my teenagers would be less than thrilled to go through this experience with a stranger.

Thankfully, everything went quickly, and she found no bruising. She told me since I had secured a restraining order against my husband, they would not take the children away from me. Praise the Lord!

I share this story as a warning: social services might be called at any time while you are living with your abusive husband. Currently, in most states, social services sees their role as the protector of children only. If they discern the children have experienced neglect, physical danger, or any other safety concern, they may take them away from *you*, citing "failure to protect." Some parents have been convicted of child abuse for failing to protect their children from abuse by the other partner.

Lifesaver from a Survivor

If social services feels you haven't protected your children from your abuser, you may lose your children, or be convicted of child abuse yourself.

In more progressive states, a movement is underway toward helping abused women move away from their abusive partners, keeping custody of their children; but, at this writing, this is certainly not the norm. Your local women's crisis center will have a good idea what your local social services is like. However, as my situation shows, what social services deems best, and what a judge in a court case may consider the best action are worlds apart. A judge might see you calling social services as a ploy to get full custody of the children, which could backfire during a divorce. As always, pray for the Lord's discernment.

Debbie's Experience

Debbie had an even more dramatic experience with social services in 1985. After a court-ordered visit with their father, Debbie's young daughters, ages two and six, talked about a game called "mailman" that their father played with them on the visit. When Debbie asked for more information, her six-year-old became defensive, and started changing her story. When the truth finally came out, Debbie learned the six-year-old had walked in on her father fondling her little sister in the bathroom. Debbie was devastated, and called a pastor's wife for advice.

They finally decided she should call the police and tell them what her daughter had said. Debbie went to the police station to make a report, and social services got involved. Social services interviewed Debbie and her daughters separately, using anatomically correct dolls to help them describe exactly what had happened. Social services also worked with the police to craft charges against her husband to take to the grand jury. Unlike my experience, Debbie felt protected and cared for in her experience with social services.

Before her husband was aware he was being investigated for molestation, he insisted on seeing the children again. Debbie's family came to monitor the visit, as was recommended by the sheriff. Even with six adults present, her husband managed to fondle the two-year-old under her shorts. When he left, the little girl asked for help in the bathroom, and told everyone what her father had done to her. Debbie immediately took her to the emergency room for an examination. They confirmed she had been sexually abused by fondling.

Debbie and her daughters then went through the trauma of the court case, where the girls had to describe what had happened to them, while their father sat just a few feet away. Currently, court hearings have more protection for minors who have been abused, but in 1985 they were not given protection. Debbie had to choose what was most important: protect-

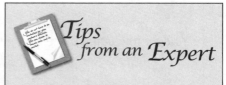

Tips from an Expert

Don't count on others when dealing with the courts. Be your own advocate, and make sure you are where you need to be.

ing her daughters from the trauma of the court proceedings, or holding her husband accountable for his actions. She decided to pursue the case, feeling that preventing him the chance to molest them, or other children, again was most important.

Unfortunately, because Debbie could not afford to hire a private attorney, she had to depend on county prosecutors to inform her when the court hearings were scheduled. Because the county attorney didn't subpoena her, and she wasn't present for her husband's trial, after he had been indicted by the grand jury, he was released from the charges of molestation.

What can we learn from this sad story? If you ever end up in a similar situation, and must depend on county prosecutors because you cannot afford your own attorney, you need to be your own advocate. Don't sit by waiting for others to inform you when hearings will be. Make sure *you* know when they will be, and that you are where *you* need to be.

1. Are you concerned the dynamics of your relationship are affecting your children? In what ways?

2. Can you think of a friend, family member, or person at church you would feel safe talking with about your marriage?

3. Could you see yourself calling the National Domestic Violence Hotline, or visiting a women's crisis center? Why or why not? What circumstance would make you willing to seek out that type of help?

4. Does the idea of making a safety plan frighten you or give you comfort?

5. Can you think of any additional items not mentioned in Chapter 10 you would want to take with you should you ever have to leave home?

6. Have you given thought to what you would do or say if your husband were to become physically abusive to you? Toward your children? Toward your pets?

7. What could you do to educate yourself about police or social services responses before you might have to deal with them?

A Drink of Water for the Journey

You are my hiding place; you will protect me from trouble

and surround me with songs of deliverance.

(Psalm 32:7)

SECTION 4:

Insisting on Change

CHAPTER 13:

How Can You Find the Courage to Ask for Change?

During the twenty years of my marriage, I tried everything I could think of to help my husband see how he was hurting me. I explained what his behavior did to me more times than I could count. What I did not really understand, until I began learning about emotional abuse, is that he *did* know he was hurting me, and he was doing it, on purpose, to control me.

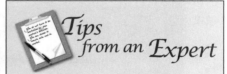

Prayer alone most likely will not change the abuse you are receiving. You will need to take responsibility to educate yourself, and create a safety plan.

Realizing this was a major turning point. At that moment, I realized I wasn't just in a difficult marriage, where things might eventually improve if I prayed hard enough. I began to realize that, instead of getting better, my husband's abuse was getting worse. I changed from being unhappy in my marriage to being afraid of my husband.

Looking back, I wish I had understood he was emotionally abusing me years earlier. As I accepted this pattern of behavior, it began to feel normal to me. Perhaps if I had asked for change earlier, before his pattern of abuse was so ingrained, our marriage might have been saved. Then again, realizing this earlier may have made no difference.

Give Yourself Time to Mourn

If you have realized you are being abused, and your husband is doing it on purpose to hurt you, give yourself some time to grieve the loss of the dream of a good marriage. Suddenly, you are awake to the reality that your marriage is not going to improve; in fact, things will continue to get worse if you don't take steps to change it. What a difficult thing to accept!

Lifesaver from a Survivor

If you have just faced the truth that you are being abused, give yourself time to grieve the loss of your dream of having a good marriage.

The following passage provided great comfort to me. In Luke 4:19, the apostle Luke records Jesus quoting from Isaiah 61. He points the Jews in his hometown to the fact that *He* is the anointed one, and He has come to free the captives. Jesus first quotes from Isaiah 61:1:

> *The Spirit of the Sovereign* LORD *is on me,*
>
> *because the* LORD *has anointed me*
>
> *to preach good news to the poor.*
>
> *He has sent me to bind up the brokenhearted,*
>
> *to proclaim freedom for the captives*
>
> *and release from darkness for the prisoners,*

In my marriage, I *did* feel like I was being held captive. I saw no way out. I had begun counting the years until I could die and go live with the Lord. What a huge relief when I realized God didn't want me to live in pain and fear. This is *not* His design for marriage. Verse two says:

> *to proclaim the year of the* LORD's *favor*
>
> *and the day of vengeance of our God,*
>
> *to comfort all who mourn,*

I was definitely in mourning for my marriage, and for my hopes and dreams of a life built with a man I thought was Christian—but these words offered me freedom, and the courage to ask for change.

Are You Worthy of Being Treated with Respect?

Another thing that may be difficult for you is to ask for change in an effective way. The purpose of your husband getting power over you is to make you feel powerless. Being called names, told you are crazy, and ignored or frightened over a long period of time can make you doubt yourself, and your perception of what is happening. You may also doubt you are worthy of being treated with respect.

> *Just because your husband claims to be a Christian does not mean he won't abuse you. Christian homes have just as much abuse as non-Christian homes.*

My husband had a way of making me feel ugly, even though others told me how beautiful I was.

Isaiah 61:3 encouraged me with a description of how God sees me:

> *and provide for those who grieve in Zion—*
>
> *to bestow on them a crown of beauty*
>
> *instead of ashes,*
>
> *the oil of gladness*
>
> *instead of mourning,*
>
> *and a garment of praise*
>
> *instead of a spirit of despair.*
>
> *They will be called oaks of righteousness,*
>
> *a planting of the LORD*
>
> *for the display of his splendor.*

I pictured myself wearing a garment of praise given by Jesus, instead of the spirit of despair my husband gave me.

Please know God sees you as His beautiful, spotless bride. You are worthy of Him sending His one and only Son to earth to die for you. As Isaiah 54:4–6 promises:

"Do not be afraid; you will not suffer shame.

Do not fear disgrace; you will not be humiliated.

You will forget the shame of your youth

and remember no more the reproach of your widowhood.

For your Maker is your husband—

the LORD Almighty is his name—

the Holy One of Israel is your Redeemer;

he is called the God of all the earth.

The LORD will call you back

as if you were a wife deserted and distressed in spirit—

a wife who married young,

only to be rejected," says your God.

You won't be alone when you ask for change. With His help, and with the resources I will discuss in the next few chapters, you can find the courage to ask for the changes needed to try saving your marriage. Jesus will walk the road with you. Jesus promises, "I have told you these things, so that in me you may have peace. In this world you will have trouble. But take heart! I have overcome the world." (John 16:33)

My hope is that, by now, you have received loving friendship, mentoring, and/or some counseling as described in Chapter 9. This will be very important to you, because asking an abuser for change is difficult, and you will want all the support you can find. Also, making a safety plan for yourself as described in Chapter 10 in case your husband's abuse escalates when he sees you are no longer willing to accept his abuse is paramount.

For this next task, you will need to arm yourself with God's power:

Finally, be strong in the LORD and in his mighty power.

Therefore put on the full armor of God, so that when the day

of evil comes, you may be able to stand your ground, and after

*you have done everything, to stand. **Stand firm** then, with the* *belt of truth buckled around your waist, with the breastplate of righteousness in place, and with your feet fitted with the readiness that comes from the gospel of peace. In addition to all this, take up the shield of faith, with which you can extinguish all the flaming arrows of the evil one.*

(Ephesians 6:10, 13-16, emphasis mine).

CHAPTER 14:

How Can Setting Boundaries Help?

One great resource for standing up to abuse is the book *Boundaries: When to Say Yes, When to Say No to Take Control of Your Life* by Dr. Henry Cloud and Dr. John Townsend, Christian psychologists.[41] They explain how relational boundaries show where I end and someone else begins, just as the boundary lines in my yard show where my property ends and my neighbor's yard begins. I am only responsible to mow, fertilize, and water the grass on my property, not that of my neighbor's.

I learned relational boundaries are also like the boundary of the skin on my body. My skin is designed to keep good things in my body, and keep potentially harmful things out of it. So, too, a relational boundary helps me keep in the good things in my life (happiness, joy, and peace, for example), and keep the bad things (pain, abuse, sorrow, and similar negatives) out.

Problems arise when one spouse tries to control the feelings, attitudes, behaviors, choices, and values of the other; things only each individual can ultimately control. To try to control these things is to violate someone's boundaries. In the end, it will fail. Any successful relationship—and our relationship with Christ—is based on freedom.

Setting boundaries with our husbands may seem anti-Christian, but in reality, having boundaries with people is quite biblical. The best example of this is God's boundaries with us. He will not allow sin to be near Him. Since we are all sinners, the only way for us to spend eternity with Him is by being washed in the sinless blood of His own Son, Jesus. We are also allowed to have boundaries with God. We are given the choice to choose Him or to say, "No, thanks." God is a gentleman; we are able to choose our response to His invitation.

Boundaries rely on the **law of sowing and reaping.** Galatians 6:7 says: "Do not be deceived: God cannot be mocked. A man reaps what he sows."

Unfortunately, in an abusive marriage, the abusive husband usually does not reap what he sows. For example, my husband used to yell at me often for no good reason. Because I feared him, I went out of my way to behave more lovingly toward him. In this case, his evil (yelling) produced good things (more loving) for him. This is not how the natural world works. In the natural world, if a farmer plants poor seed, he receives a poor crop.

The way to begin using the law of reaping and sowing in an abusive marriage is to allow the husband to receive the natural consequences of his behavior. For example, you could tell your overly critical husband if he continues berating you, you will go into another room until he can discuss the problem rationally. Or, you could say, "If you start yelling at me again, I will go to Jane's house to spend the night." In this way, you would be letting your out-of-control husband suffer the consequences of his actions. This move is not manipulative, though he would probably accuse you of trying to manipulate him. Rather, this response is simply an example of limiting how you allow yourself to be treated. The natural consequences are then falling on the shoulders of the responsible party.

Before I learned about boundaries, I might have said something like, "You've just got to stop yelling. It's ruining our family. Please listen. You're wrecking our lives." *After* I learned about boundaries, I might say, "You may choose to not deal with your behavior if you want, but I will not continue to expose myself and the children to this chaos. The next time you begin raging, we will go to the Wilsons' for the night, and we will tell them why we are there. Your behavior is your choice. What I will put up with is mine."[42]

> *"We train people how to treat us."* If we allow people to treat us badly, they will.

As this example shows, a boundary always deals with you, not with the other person. You cannot demand your spouse do something, or even respect your boundaries. You are setting boundaries to say what you will do or will not do. Only these kinds of boundaries are enforceable, for you only have control over yourself. Do not confuse boundaries with a way to control your spouse. It is the opposite. It is giving up control, and beginning to love. You are giving up trying to control your spouse, and allowing him to take responsibility for his own behavior.

Don't Try to Start Building Boundaries Alone

Beginning to set boundaries with an abusive husband can be difficult and frightening. The fear of abandonment keeps many people from setting boundaries, even with "easy" people. For this reason, establishing a support system of people who will encourage boundary setting in your marriage is very important. Do not set boundaries alone. You have not set boundaries because you are afraid; the only way out is through support. Ecclesiastes 4:12 says, "Though one may be overpowered, two can defend themselves. A cord of three strands is not quickly broken."

> *Remember . . .*
>
> *Boundaries are like muscles. They need to be built up in a safe environment and allowed to grow. If you try to shoulder too much weight too quickly, your muscles may tear or be pulled. Get help when you build boundaries.*

Boundaries are like muscles. They need to be built up in a safe environment and allowed to grow. If you try to shoulder too much weight too quickly, your muscles may tear or be pulled. Get help. This is where your friends, mentors, and counselors can help you be strong, and support you while you are changing your patterns of relating to your abusive husband; a very difficult task.

Dealing with the Other Person's Reaction

One thing I learned from my study of *Boundaries* is this: The hard part for me (and many women) in saying "no" to someone is living with their reaction. We are so used to being people pleasers that we don't like when someone is mad at us. Therefore, we spend a lot of time and energy trying to "fix it" for the other person, when this is something they need to fix themselves. We need to hold onto our "no," and let them deal with their problem accepting it.[43] Setting boundaries is my responsibility. How they react is theirs. If someone truly loves me, they will *want* to behave better and work to live within my new boundaries. Most likely, an abusive husband will not accept my new boundaries.

If you become frightened by your husband at any point when trying to set boundaries with him, Cloud and Townsend encourage you to remove yourself to get away from danger, and put limits on evil. They say:

> "The Bible urges us to separate from those who continue to hurt us and to create a safe place for ourselves. Removing yourself from the situation will also cause the one who is left behind to experience a loss of fellowship that may lead to

changed behavior. When a relationship is abusive, many times the only way to finally show the other person that your boundaries are real is to create space until they are ready to deal with the problem."[44]

The Bible supports the idea of limiting togetherness for the sake of "binding evil." Psalm 141:4, 9–10 says:

> *Let not my heart be drawn to what is evil,*
>
> > *to take part in wicked deeds*
> >
> > *with men who are evildoers;*
> >
> > *let me not eat of their delicacies.*
>
> *Keep me from the snares they have laid for me,*
>
> > *from the traps set by evildoers.*
> >
> > *Let the wicked fall into their own nets,*
> >
> > *while I pass by in safety.*

And Psalm 37:27 says:

> *Turn from evil and do good;*
>
> > *then you will dwell in the land forever.*

Note that *Boundaries* is not written specifically for abused women. We will talk more about the possibility of separating from an abusive husband, and how to safely do that in future chapters.

CHAPTER 15:

Do Boundaries Conflict with Biblical Submission in Marriage?

You might feel uncomfortable with the idea of setting boundaries with your husband. You might think, "This doesn't sound very submissive." In Chapter 5, we read Ephesians 5:21–33 for the apostle Paul's description of marital submission. God's definition is often different from the definition of submission an abusive husband might use.

In order to understand whether using boundaries with your husband might be in conflict with biblical submission, look at whether the way your husband is treating you is in line with what the Bible teaches.

In his book *Marriage, Divorce, and Remarriage in the Bible*, Jay Adams defines marriage as a "Covenant of Companionship."[45] He says a spouse is supposed to be someone with whom he (she) can talk things over, someone to counsel, someone to care—to share joys, perplexities, ideas, fears, sorrows, and disappointments—a helper. A marriage companion is someone with whom one can let down his/her hair. Marriage is meant to be the closest, most intimate of all human relationships. Two persons may begin to think, act, and feel as one.

The relationship Jay Adams describes is not the description of an abusive marriage. In an abusive relationship no oneness of spirit, no openness, and no equality exists. Because of the abusive way the husband treats his wife, he is breaking the Covenant of Companionship the Lord designed marriage to be. He is, therefore, committing sin against you.

As I explained in Chapter 7, you are

> *God designed marriage as a "Covenant of Companionship."*
>
> *In an abusive relationship, your husband is breaking this covenant. Therefore, he is committing sin against God, and against you. The Lord grieves to see you treated disrespectfully.*

God's bride. You are more precious to Him than you could ever imagine. God desires for all marriages to be havens of support and love for everyone in the family, as we saw described in Ephesians 5:25–33. Therefore, the Lord grieves to see you treated disrespectfully and abusively. This is not His ultimate desire for you.

Let us turn now from theory to ask pertinent questions about your marriage:

- **Is your husband following Paul's advice in Ephesians 5:25 and loving you like Christ loves the church?** In an abusive marriage, this is probably not the case. Do you live in freedom, or must you live as a slave to his whims and rules? Galatians 3:23 says, "Before this faith came, we were held prisoners by the law, locked up until faith should be revealed."

- **Do you feel as if you live under the law, locked up?** When your husband tries to keep you "under the law," you will feel all the emotions the Bible promises living under the law brings: wrath, guilt, insecurity, and alienation (Romans 4:15, James 2:10, Galatians 5:4). In my own marriage, I felt all these emotions on a regular basis. When my husband raged at me for being a "terrible wife" by not meeting his expectations, my first response was justifiable anger. After some time, I would begin to feel guilty for being angry. I would ask myself, "Doesn't the Bible say not to let the sun go down on your anger?" (Ephesians 4:26). Yet, because my husband would not let me express my anger or discuss *my* issues or concerns about our relationship, I went to bed angry night after night. Soon, my anger and guilt led me to feel insecure not only in my husband's love, but more importantly, in the Lord's love. At times, this led me to feel alienated from both of them—my husband and my Lord.

  > *Our anger, guilt, and confusion may lead us to feel alienated from God.*

- **Are you experiencing grace and freedom in your marriage?** Usually husbands who quote Ephesians 5 turn their wives into slaves and condemn them for not submitting. If you incur wrath or condemnation for not submitting, you and your husband do not have a grace-filled Christian marriage; instead, you have a marriage "under the law."

- **Does your husband demonstrate he loves you as much as he loves his own body?** Ephesians 5:28–29 says, " . . . husbands ought to love their wives as their own bodies. He who loves his wife loves himself. After all, no one ever hated his own body, but he feeds and cares for it, just as Christ does the church." When your husband treats you with a lack of respect, he sins against not only God, but against himself. The Bible has no reference to a slave-like submission. Christ never takes away our will or demands we do something we don't want to. He is a gentleman, and He treats us gently. He never uses us as objects; instead, He "gave himself up" (Ephesians 5:25) for us. He takes care of us as He would His own body.

Cloud and Townsend don't believe that boundaries are insubmissive. They explain:

"We have never seen a 'submission problem' that did not have a controlling husband at its root. When the wife begins to set clear boundaries, the lack of Christ-likeness in a controlling husband becomes evident because the wife is no longer enabling his immature behavior. She is confronting the truth and setting biblical limits on hurtful behavior. Often, when the wife sets boundaries, the husband begins to grow up."[46]

I will describe specific ways to start setting boundaries with an abusive husband in the next Chapter.

CHAPTER 16:

In What Other Ways Can You Insist upon Change?

In this Chapter, I will outline some methods for you to ask for change in your husband's abusive behavior, based upon *The Verbally Abusive Relationship* by Patricia Evans.[47] This book was not written from a Christian point of view, so I will add my perspective as a Christian woman.

God has called all wives to be respectful to their husbands, as Paul writes in Ephesians 5:22-24. However, allowing your husband to be disrespectful to *you* is not the way to show *him* respect. Nor are you showing him love by allowing him to continue his abusive behavior. God wants him to change, to be the loving, sacrificial husband described in Ephesians 5:25-33. Most likely, one of the reasons you have allowed his abuse in the past was to protect *yourself* because you have been afraid of his anger. Protecting yourself is *not* doing what is best for your husband. After all, Paul writes to the Ephesians in verses 4:14-16:

> *Then we will no longer be infants, tossed back and forth*
>
> *by the waves, and blown here and there by every wind of*
>
> *teaching and by the cunning and craftiness of men in their*
>
> *deceitful scheming. Instead, speaking the truth in love,*
>
> *we will in all things grow up into him who is the Head,*
>
> *that is, Christ. From him the whole body, joined and held*
>
> *together by every supporting ligament, grows and*
>
> *builds itself up in love, as each part does its work.*

So, how *should* you go about asking him to change?

Start Setting Limits
Your husband probably has many behaviors which bother and upset

you. You will first want to think through those behaviors and decide which ones you are no longer willing to accept. Some examples might be:

1. Calling you names[48]
2. Yelling at you
3. Ordering you around as if you were his servant
4. Threatening you
5. Accusing you and blaming you
6. Judging and criticizing you
7. Making a joke at your expense
8. Withholding finances
9. Keeping you from resources (such as cars, phones, computers)
10. Telling you how to dress or act, or
11. Any other behavior designed to hurt you or make you angry

Once you have decided what you are no longer willing to accept, then you need to call him on those behaviors every time he does it. When you do this, speaking firmly so he knows you are not joking around would be wise. Be sure to behave respectfully to him, as Paul suggests in Ephesians 5:22–24, though.

Practicing what you will say before you are in a difficult situation with your husband is a good idea. For example, you might need to say:

Lifesaver from a Survivor

Learn to say to the abuser in a firm voice, "Stop it." Do not explain yourself, your needs, or what you mean. Simply call a halt to the abuse, and let that be your final word.

- "I will not accept being called names."
- "I will not accept you yelling at me."
- "I will not allow you to order me around."
- "I will not accept you blaming me."
- "I will not accept you criticizing or judging me."

- "I will not accept comments or 'jokes' that put me down."

- . . . and other statements applicable to your unique situation.

If, at the moment of abuse, you are speechless, you can train yourself to say in a firm voice, "Stop it."

Your goal will be to say something about every offensive thing your husband tries to do. When you do this in a firm tone of voice, you will be letting him know you mean what you say. Do not explain yourself, your needs, or what you mean. That is probably how you have responded in the past, and it most likely didn't work. Responding that way gives him more fuel with which to continue abusing you, and keeps you stuck in the same old patterns. Simply call a halt to the abuse, and let that be your final word.

Be Prepared for His Reaction

Be prepared for his reaction. You do not know how he will react. A husband who is not a confirmed abuser, or who is willing to make changes for you, may immediately back down, or at least consider what you are saying. On the other hand, a true abuser will likely get angrier, because he sees he is losing control over you. Since the purpose of his abuse is to gain control, when he sees he is beginning to lose that control, he will not like it.

How he reacts will help you to determine whether your husband is willing, or even able, to stop abusing you. I did not try this step until I had been severely abused over many years. At that point, my husband was a confirmed abuser. He was very hostile toward me, and I was afraid of him. I wish now I had educated myself about emotional abuse years before. He might have been more willing to change had I tried this approach earlier. I recommend trying this as soon as possible in your marriage. Don't wait until things are unbearable before seeking change. The sooner the better!

When you begin to set limits, you have to give up your usual ways of keeping the peace in your home. Maybe you have tried to explain how his behavior makes you feel. Maybe you have tried to understand why he would treat you this way. Maybe you have wracked your brain trying to figure out what you did wrong, or how you can be perfect enough, so he will never be angry with you again. Most likely, you have done all these things over and over for a long period of time. By now, you are probably realizing he doesn't care how his behavior makes you feel, and you can never be perfect enough to make him stop abusing you. In fact, if you are generally a respectful, caring wife, *nothing* you do can make him treat you with respect unless you insist on it.

Be prepared for your husband to suddenly act like the injured party. For example, he might say, "I'm just telling you the truth because I love you," or "I can't believe you would be that disrespectful to me," or "You always need to win an argument," or "I never said that," or any number of things. However, you know he is not abusing you because he loves you, you are not being disrespectful, you are not trying to win an argument, and, in fact, he *did* say that! Ask the Lord to help you to *stand firm* in this difficult situation. 1 Corinthians 16:13–14 says:

*Be on your guard; **stand firm** in the faith; be men of courage;*

be strong. Do everything in love.

(emphasis mine)

Remember, allowing your husband to continue abusing you is not showing him God's love.

Be Prepared for Difficulties as You Try to Make Changes

So . . . you are ready to take the potentially dangerous, but necessary, risk of trying to make changes in your abusive marriage. Look out for these potential bumps in the road:

1. **Guilt:** You may feel guilty about talking to someone about the abuse, since you have probably been blamed for the abuse. You may even feel guilty for learning about emotional abuse.

2. **Insecurity:** You may have been conditioned to feel wrong about setting limits and refusing to accept abuse.

3. **Denial:** Once you begin setting limits, your husband may continue to strongly deny he has done anything wrong. If you have grown accustomed to believing everything he says about himself, and about you, you may have difficulty believing your own perception of what is happening. Accepting your own perceptions and feelings is critical. Ask the Lord to help you see the truth about what is happening. 2 Timothy 1:7 says:

For God did not give us a spirit of timidity, but a spirit of power,

of love and of self-discipline.

4. **Self-doubt:** If the abuse you've experienced has occurred primarily in private, you may think you are misreading his

actions. You may truly think something is wrong with you because no one else is around to say "Hey, that's abusive!" Or, you may think your husband has no idea what he is doing. If this is the case, remember that *most crimes are committed in secret.* Just as a thief knows what he is doing in secret, the abuser knows what he is doing in secret. He may not understand what compels him, but if he continues to deny the abuse, is unwilling to discuss the abuse, and remains hostile toward you, he has become a confirmed abuser. Unless a person or circumstances cause him to reevaluate his life and actions, he is unlikely to make any lasting changes. This is where holding a man accountable for his actions comes in. We will look at this in detail in Chapter 18.

5. **Grief:** Another difficulty you may have is realizing you are the primary, and perhaps only, person he is abusing. You may then ask yourself, "Why would he do this to me?" You may also have to accept the loss of the illusion that your marriage is fine and will improve on its own. This is a real loss, similar to a death. While I've already suggested in Chapter 13 you give yourself time to grieve, let me go a step farther and say grief is a bump in the road you need not fear. Take this pain to the Lord. Be honest with Him about all your feelings: shock, hatred, fear, sadness, hopelessness, and worthlessness, whatever they might be. Also, now is the time to really lean on your friends, counselors, and mentors; in other words, the support system you have created for yourself. One thing I learned very late in my situation is people will not stop loving me if they find I am weak, struggling, unhappy, or angry. I wore a pretend happy face for the world to see for a very long time. I finally realized by not accepting my own grief I was unable to be compassionate to others who were struggling. Also, my "happy face" kept me distant from those who were willing to love and care for me, and I could have really benefitted from their love and care.

6. **Danger:** Finally, and most upsetting, your husband may very well intensify his abuse. If you become afraid of him, or if he becomes physically violent, put your safety plan into action and leave, at least temporarily.

If you have not yet done so after reading Chapter 10, I strongly encourage you to make a safety plan for you and your children before you begin asking for change. A confirmed abuser can become angrier and violent when faced with resistance to his abuse. Even if you have not prepared for this, you have every right to leave a dangerous situation and take your children and pets with you.

When you are away from home with your husband, carry enough money with you at all times so you can get home from wherever you are. Also, have your personal phone book with you so you can call a friend if you need a ride. When I became very frightened of my husband, my personal phone book became my lifeline. At times, I was so upset I could not think of the phone number of my best friend, who I called all the time. Do not count on having your cell phone with you. He may take it or destroy it.

As mentioned above, keep a bag packed in your car if you have one, or else in a safe place you can easily get to at any moment. Plan ahead where and how you will go if you need to leave your house.

A Word About the Abuse of Withholding

One category of abuse will not be helped by standing firm and telling your husband to "stop it." That category of abuse is called *withholding*. I am very familiar with this type of abuse because this was my husband's favorite tool. Earlier in our marriage, he would do this for a day or two at a time. Toward the end of the marriage, he would withhold for a month at a time. The last year of our marriage, he withheld for an entire year.

So, what is withholding? An abuser withholds any kind of affection or attention to his mate. He keeps all his thoughts, feelings, hopes, and dreams to himself. He may completely ignore his wife, to the point of not responding to her if she speaks directly to him, or stepping around her if she goes near him, as if she does not physically exist. My husband used to ask the children at the dinner table to pass him the ketchup next to me, as if I were not physically present. If your husband is a withholder, you know the extreme pain of living with someone like this.

Telling an extreme withholder to "stop it" will do no good at all, since he does not acknowledge your existence. Patricia Evans says withholding is a violation of your boundaries,[49] and you need not accept this behavior. She recommends you leave your husband's presence, saying matter-of-factly, "I am feeling very bored with your company." Then, you can be gone as long as you wish. You can read a book, visit a friend, or take your kids on an outing. Anything you do will be less boring or painful than sitting through the silent treatment. I tried things like this, but it made no impact on my husband whatsoever. Perhaps it will have more impact on yours.

As we saw in Chapter 15, Jay Adams's definition of marriage is a covenant of companionship two people make with each other. A man who is withholding affection and companionship from his wife is breaking the covenant he made with her, just as a man who berates his wife and expects her to never make him angry is breaking his covenant with her.

A husband who is abusing his wife is sinning against her by breaking his marriage covenant. If he refuses to change once she has asked for change privately, she may then turn to others for help in asking for change.

1. Do you believe God truly sees you as a spotless bride, someone worth sending His Son to die for?

2. Do you think using boundaries so your husband could reap what he sows would be helpful? Why or why not?

3. If your husband has been sinning by breaking the covenant of companionship that marriage is supposed to be, do you think setting boundaries with his behavior is unbiblical? Why or why not?

4. How do you think you would feel when you start setting limits with your husband as described in Chapter 16?

5. What things can you do to prepare yourself for his reactions when you begin setting limits with him?

A Drink of Water for the Journey

. . . as a bridegroom rejoices over his bride, so will your God rejoice over you.

(Isaiah 62:5b)

CHAPTER 16: In What Other Ways Can You Insist upon Change?

SECTION 5:

Assessing the Changes You've Asked For

CHAPTER 17:

How Can You Tell if He Has *Really* Changed?

This is a good question to ask. At first, determining whether he has really changed or whether he is just going through the motions of another "honeymoon" stage is difficult.

The Honeymoon Stage

Emotional abuse comes in cycles, which I described in detail in Chapter 2. The first phase is the explosive or abusive stage, which is often (but not always) followed by the honeymoon stage. During the honeymoon stage, your husband will behave very lovingly toward you, and usually make a lot of promises about changing his behavior. This stage of the abuse cycle is when he will say things like, "Oh, that was wrong of me. Don't worry, that will *never* happen again. You know I love you so much, I can't live without you," or some similar declaration. The honeymoon stage is usually followed by the tension building stage, and then another explosive stage occurs.

If your husband is in a honeymoon stage, he has not had a true realization that he has been treating you abusively. Emotional abuse will not disappear overnight. In order to stop this habit, your husband will have to commit to some serious, difficult work over a long period of time. He will need to realize, remember, and admit to what he has done in the past. He will have to recognize and have empathy for what you have endured. He will need to understand what is causing him to behave this way, and make a serious commitment to ending those behaviors. You will both find this process difficult.

Since domestic violence flourishes in secret, one sign he has changed is when he will no longer try to hide his abuse. As Proverbs 28:13 says:

He who conceals his sins does not prosper, but whoever

confesses and renounces them finds mercy.

If your husband truly realizes he has sinned by emotionally abusing you, he will freely confess it to others and renounce his former behavior. In addition, you should notice him seeking help on his own to correct this problem. He might be:

- Reading books about emotional abuse,
- Seeking accountability partners, and/or
- Meeting weekly with a counselor who is trained to deal with abusive men.

If He Really Has Changed, He Should Enroll in a Treatment Program for Abusers

One thing you should *insist* on is that he enrolls in a group treatment program for abusers. Call the National Domestic Violence Hotline for information about programs in your area; many cities have treatment programs for abusive men.

Abuse treatment programs are unlike any other type of counseling he might receive. Your husband will be assigned to the program for a set period of time depending on how he has treated you in the past. The time period may be at least nine months. The treatment provider will be trained to deal with abusers, and will usually be able to see through lies he may try to tell about his current or past behaviors. Although many of these groups are not specifically Christian, they may have Christian counselors on staff.

During his time in the program, a victim's advocate representing the treatment program will be available to speak with you about concerns you have regarding your relationship with your husband. These groups are designed to hold your husband accountable for his actions no matter what he claims "provoked" his behavior. They work to change his attitudes, and teach him other ways to express anger besides being abusive. They should help him explore underlying problems he may have had in his early life that allow him to feel it is acceptable to abuse you.

Very few abusers forced into domestic violence treatment are initially happy to attend them. However, many abusers begin to recognize their abusive behaviors, and work toward changing them. Most of the men in these programs have been forced by the courts, by a partner, or employer who has given him an ultimatum. Others may finish the program, but not take it seriously, giving the counselors lip service. If your husband takes the course seriously, and finishes the program, you have a greater chance of repairing your marriage.

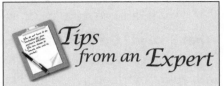

Tips from an Expert

Your husband's abuse of you feels "normal" to him. A goal of the treatment program is to teach a healthier normal for the relationship.

If He Really *Has* Changed, What Should *We* Do Differently in the Future?

Once your husband has gone through domestic violence treatment, he should have learned more effective skills in managing his anger and his relationships. You will also have to continue with the changes you have been making, such as watching your own reactions and setting respectful boundaries with him. You also have to do some difficult work healing from the abuse you've experienced, and learning to forgive your husband.

Detective Sgt. Donald Stewart is a police sergeant who has specialized in domestic violence cases for twenty-five years. His book *Refuge: A Pathway Out of Domestic Violence and Abuse* looks at domestic violence from a policeman's point of view. This is a summary of his advice for couples who manage to stay together after abuse has left their relationship:[50]

1. If either you or your husband are used to drinking alcohol or doing drugs, that person must stop immediately.

2. If you have been hanging around with the bar or casino crowd, get some new friends who are not involved in that lifestyle. 1 Corinthians 15:33 says:

> *Do not be misled: "Bad company corrupts good character."*

3. If you have been watching pornography alone or together, get rid of it, and never allow it in your home again.

What Should I Do If My Abuser is My Boyfriend?

Sgt. Stewart has some tough advice if you are in a sexual relationship with your boyfriend. He says, "Having a sexually intimate relationship with your boyfriend is prohibited by God—it is sin. God prohibits sex outside of marriage. Either marry him or get rid of him. My advice is to get rid of him as soon as it's safe to do so. Any man who lives with his girlfriend doesn't love her according to God's standard. Cut off all sex to him and tell him, 'No more until we're married.' See how long he sticks around. He's simply test-driving to see if he wants to keep you. I guarantee you that as soon as you don't look quite good enough, fail to live up to his expectations, or start to cause him a little discomfort or inconvenience, you're history. Love is a commitment, not a test drive. God will not bless an intimate relationship outside of marriage."

I agree with the sergeant. If your boyfriend really loves you, he will not cause you to sin in the Lord's eyes. You *might* consider marrying him after a year has passed *if* he is willing to:

* Move out of your house (if he lives there),

* Stop having sex with you,

* Stay faithful to you,

* Get help to change his abusive ways by entering domestic violence treatment, and

* Be held accountable for his abusive behaviors.

Waiting a year gives you time to determine if he has really changed. If he does not make all of these changes, I would get rid of him, if it is safe to do so. We will talk more about how to leave him safely in Chapters 26 through 28.

CHAPTER 18:

How Can You Confront Your Husband if He Hasn't Changed?

At this point, you have hopefully taken the following steps:

1. Examined your own behavior and motives in your relationship, and changed any behaviors of yours you believe are displeasing to the Lord.

2. You are aware of a continuing pattern of abuse in your relationship, and you have examined your values and beliefs about the impact of the abuse on you and your children.

3. You have educated yourself about domestic violence via books, the Internet, counselors, and support groups.

4. You have acquired a support system of friends who will pray for you and support your safety.

5. You have spent quite a bit of time standing firm and setting boundaries against the abuse to let your husband know you will no longer accept abuse from him.

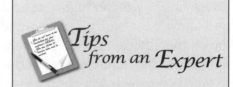

Tips from an Expert

Many Christian women will turn to their church first. Please recognize not all churches are equipped to deal with such sensitive and potentially dangerous circumstances. Be thoughtful about where you ask for help. You may have to look in more than one place.

The Process as Described in Matthew 18

What if, after you've done all this, your husband refuses to change, or his abuse gets even worse? Does a Christian woman have any recourse? After all, no woman, especially a Christian woman, wants to be divorced.

Is that your only option now? Thankfully, you can do something else. Jesus outlined this process in Matthew 18:15–17:

"If your brother sins against you, go and show him his fault,

just between the two of you. If he listens to you, you have

won your brother over. But if he will not listen, take one or two

others along, so that 'every matter may be established by the

testimony of two or three witnesses.' If he refuses to listen to

them, tell it to the church; and if he refuses to listen even to the

church, treat him as you would a pagan or a tax collector."

In verse 15, Jesus talks about your brother sinning against you. Emotional abuse is sin. This is not God's plan for marriage. Once we accept abuse is sin, we can follow Jesus's instructions here. He says to first go and show your brother his fault, just between the two of you. If you followed the advice outlined in Chapter 16, you have already shown him his fault while still behaving respectfully toward him. Jesus says, "If he listens to you, you have won your brother over," which I described in Chapter 17.

What if Your Husband is Not Committed to Changing His Behavior?

This is the time to ask yourself whether your husband is truly committed to changing his behavior. If he is, he will show true repentance, and significant changes will occur in his life. But what if your husband is not committed to changing his behavior? If he continues to go through abusive cycles with no real evidence of a change of heart, Jesus tells us to seek help from others. In Matthew 18:16 he says:

" But if he will not listen, take one or two others along,

so that 'every matter may be established

by the testimony of two or three witnesses.'"

Before you take this step, you should ask yourself if you are prepared to follow through with this course of action. This is a critical step, and it may lead to the end of your marriage. Your husband may choose not to forgive you for "causing" the embarrassment or shame of having his actions known publicly. Be aware the safety of all involved should be the first priority. Only seek the help of friends or church leaders if you believe your husband's reaction would not put others in danger. If you have concerns about safety, you should turn to law enforcement for help instead.

If you *are* ready to move forward, and bring in the help of others, who are the one or two others you should take along? If your husband has godly male friends he looks up to, you could begin by appealing to them for help. Talk with them first to see if they will keep your confidence until you are ready to act. Asking the following questions of them first would be wise:

1. Do they understand what the role of a husband should be, and do they agree that your husband's behavior is sin, and unacceptable?

2. Will they agree to hold him accountable for his actions?

3. Will they protect you if your husband's anger escalates? (This is a very real possibility.)

4. Will they ask him to leave if he becomes violent?

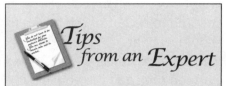

Tips from an Expert

The safety of all involved should be your first priority. If you believe your husband's reaction might put others in danger, turn to law enforcement for help instead.

5. Will they take you with them, or are they willing to call the police, if you are frightened about staying with your husband?

If the answer to any of the above questions is no, these are not the right people to ask for help.

Many abusive men do not have close friends. They often have only superficial relationships, or no relationships at all. If this is the case, you may need to ask the husbands of one or two of your close friends to assist you. Many abusers isolate their wives. Because of this, you may not have any close friends. In this case, you may need to confide in someone at your church. Whomever you choose, make sure they understand what is happening in your home. They could probably benefit from some education about emotional abuse. You could offer to let them read this book, or suggest *The Verbally Abusive Relationship* by Patricia Evans or *Why Does He DO That?* by Lundy Bancroft. Or you could recommend some of the websites I have listed in the Appendix of this book. Once they have some education, make sure they are also willing to do whatever is required to help you.

Confronting Your Husband with His Abuse

Should you go along with the men who have agreed to speak to your husband? Or should they speak to him without you present? This is *your* decision. If you feel comfortable, you may decide going with them is the best course of action. This way, your husband will not be able to tell them a story that is not true, or if he does, you will be able to counter it. If you are afraid of your husband's reaction, you may want to plan for you and your children to be out of the house for a few days. During those few days, you should evaluate his reaction. Is he angry with you? Is he showing signs of true repentance, as we discussed in Chapter 17? Is he going into the honeymoon phase of the abuse cycle?

I have heard of men who immediately feel repentant when a friend confronts them about their behavior. This is, of course, what every abused woman would hope for. If your husband truly is repentant about his behavior, and is willing to work to change his life, what a blessing! Of course, discerning whether or not he is making false promises, like he probably has many times in the past during honeymoon phases, is challenging. If he is truly repentant, you will clearly notice, over a long period of time (months and years), changed behavior.

In this first meeting with his friends, ask them to outline steps he should take to get the help he needs. These steps are:

1. Meet with these friends weekly, to hold him accountable. They will want to speak to you weekly as well, to verify what he is saying to them.

2. Work weekly with a counselor *who is trained* in dealing with abusive men.

3. Join a treatment group for male abusers (as described in Chapter 17).

Do some research about counselors and support groups in your area before bringing others to meet with your husband. Find one or two possible counselors (hopefully men), and get information about treatment programs for abusers in your area. Call the National Domestic Violence Hotline for information about programs in your area. Have names and phone numbers available for him. Ask his friends to insist on concrete steps your husband agrees to take, and then make sure they hold him accountable for following through.

1. Have you experienced the honeymoon stage before? What behaviors does your husband exhibit during the honeymoon stage?

2. What changes would your husband need to make to prove to you he has really changed? What changes would *you* need to make if you were to stay together?

3. Can you think of any men you would feel comfortable seeking help from?

A Drink of Water for the Journey

Put all things to the test: keep what is good and avoid every kind of evil.

(1 Thessalonians 5:21-22) GNT

4. What preparations would you want to make beforehand?

5. Would you want to go with them when they speak to him?

6. What steps would you want them to take to hold him accountable?

SECTION 6:

Turning to Your Church for Help

CHAPTER 19:

If You Have Asked for Change, and He Hasn't Changed, What Next?

At this point, you have hopefully taken the following steps:

1. Examined your own behavior and motives in your relationship, and changed any of your behaviors you believe are displeasing to the Lord.

2. You are aware of a continuing pattern of abuse in your relationship, and you have examined your values and beliefs about the impact of the abuse on you and your children.

3. You have educated yourself about domestic violence via books, the Internet, counselors, and support groups.

4. You have acquired a support system of friends who will pray for you and support your safety.

5. You have spent quite a bit of time standing firm and setting boundaries against the abuse to let your husband know you will no longer accept abuse.

6. Asked two appropriate men to confront your husband and hold him accountable for changing his behavior, as Jesus instructs in Matthew 18:16.

I pray your husband has admitted his sin, is repentant, and is taking many steps to change his behavior. If not, you will need to move forward.

Should You Speak to Someone in Your Church for Help?

If you have gotten to this point, you will have performed the first two steps in the "Matthew 18" process. You will have shown him his fault between just the two of you, and you will have brought two appropriate others along as witnesses. Next, Matthew 18:17a says:

"If he refuses to listen to them, tell it to the church;"

If your husband is still abusing you, Jesus says in Matthew 18:17 that you should tell the church. This does not mean stand in front of the church and tell the *entire* congregation. It does mean finding an appropriate leader, such as one of the pastors or elders, and telling them what is happening.

This may or may not be the best step for your situation. Some churches will not be helpful to you because of lack of knowledge about domestic violence, or because of the way they interpret the Bible's description of Christian submission in marriage.

Here are some questions to consider when determining the mindset of your church's leadership regarding domestic violence:

1. Have you ever heard anything about domestic violence mentioned from the pulpit?

2. When the pastor discusses marriage relationships in his sermons, does he challenge men to love their wives as Jesus does the Church, or does he only focus on wives submitting to their husbands?

3. Do you see any materials about domestic violence posted around the church?

4. Has the church ever held any classes about domestic violence?

If you feel the leadership of your church is generally supportive of women, but you have never seen nor heard anything specific about domestic violence, you may still decide to approach them for help. This is your decision; trust your own feelings about this.

How to Find the Right Person to Approach for Help

If you *do* decide that bringing your problem to someone at your church is the right thing, be aware this is a serious step. Your husband may become so embarrassed or ashamed that he will insist on leaving the church. Or he may become violent. This is a risk you may decide to take.

If you do, finding the right person in the church to help you is essential. Most people in the general population have not been trained in how to handle domestic violence, and this is certainly true of people in the church. Many Christians will tell an abused woman to "pray harder" or "submit" to her husband, thinking that will resolve the abuse problem. It won't.

Because of this, search for a person with the following qualities:

- This person should be in a position of leadership, such as a pastor, elder, or church counselor.

- This person should be a man, because your husband will not want to listen to a woman.

- This man should have a good relationship with his wife; one where she is honored and valued as an equal partner in the marriage.

- He should be a humble man, one who is not conceited, and who has a teachable spirit.

Then ask a friend to confidentially speak to this person first so your identity is protected, until you decide if he is the correct person to appeal to. Here are some questions to have your friend ask him:

1. When you first come to meet with him, will he allow someone to come with you to support you, such as a mentor or a crisis center counselor?

2. What has he and/or the church done to help women in abusive relationships before?

3. Would he be willing to educate himself on abuse before you meet?

4. Does he agree emotional abuse is dangerous, and needs to be stopped before it becomes physical abuse?

5. Is he prepared to believe you, no matter how persuasive your husband may be?

6. Will he keep your conversation strictly confidential?[51] If and when he speaks to your husband, he must promise *not* to tell him *anything* you have disclosed. Your safety depends on this. Caution him to neither confirm nor deny what you have told him. Instead, he should focus on how your husband perceives your relationship, and remind him of his obligations to provide a safe, loving home for his family.

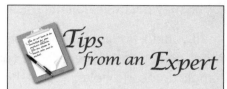

Tips from an Expert

You don't need to feel ashamed about what is happening in your home. Domestic violence thrives in secret. Keeping this secret will keep you in bondage. However, choosing a person who is safe and appropriate to help you is a vital step. Find the right person before disclosing your identity.

7. Would the church be willing to hold your husband accountable for his actions?

8. Would the church be willing to remove your husband from his leadership positions in the church (if any)?

9. Would he be willing to talk with your husband about enrolling in a program for men who abuse?

10. Would he be willing to support you if you feel you should separate from your husband for a time while he receives the help he needs?

11. If you become frightened about your husband's reaction, would he ask your husband to leave the house, or be willing to get you and your children to a safe place?

12. If things do not get better, and in fact get worse (which is a real possibility), what does the church believe are acceptable grounds for legal separation or divorce?

My Personal Experience Seeking Help at My Church

During the last few years of my marriage, I sought help from two different pastors at my church. Unfortunately, neither one was able to give my husband and me the help we needed. The first pastor was an elderly gentleman who completely understood what I told him. He offered to pray for me, but he did not offer to follow up with my husband.

A year and a half later, things had become much more frightening for me. So, even though the first pastor was not helpful, I decided to speak to a different pastor at the church. This was a person my husband knew and liked, at least on a superficial, social level. Unfortunately, I did not choose the right person.

While this pastor agreed my husband's behavior was not right, I don't think he truly believed what I told him was the truth. My husband, like many abusers, was a very charming and persuasive person. He was able to convince our pastor the actual truth of the situation was somewhere between what I said and what he said. My pastor lacked training in dealing with domestic violence, and seemed to have no real desire to educate himself about it.

I later learned I could have appealed to other men in the church who would have understood me, would have believed me, and (hopefully) would have taken the necessary steps. Unfortunately, I did not understand this at the time. I was so frightened and unnerved that I did not choose wisely who to appeal to. Please do not make the same mistake!

Debbie's First Experience Seeking Help from the Church

Debbie says she "had too much pride to listen to her dad" while he walked her down the aisle on her wedding day. He said, "It is not too late. We can leave now!" She said, "No, I made a commitment, and I will honor my commitment." She had only been a Christian for a couple of years, and believed she was called to be a pastor's wife at the age of eleven.

She later learned many people thought her wedding was a mistake, including the pastor who married them. Within twenty-four hours of their marriage, she also knew she had made a big mistake. A few months later, during her first pregnancy, she asked the wife of the pastor of their church, "Where do you go when you are married, and you are in pain?" She answered, "Once you are married, you are married. You really can't do anything." Debbie went home feeling hopeless and alone. She believed if she left her marriage, God would leave her. Debbie stayed in the marriage ten more years. During that time, her husband's emotional abuse escalated greatly. He also began taking photos of teenaged girls, and cheated on her with their teenaged babysitter, who became pregnant.

CHAPTER 20:

What Is a Good Outcome of Telling the Church?

The best possible outcome of telling the church would be the church supporting you, and helping you remain safe, while holding your husband accountable for his actions. If this *did* happen, you might have hope of saving your marriage, or at least you and your children would be able to live safely.

The church's response would take two major focuses: what they do for you, and what they do for your husband. For you, they would hopefully:[52]

1. Believe you.

2. Protect your confidentiality.

    a. Not disclose to your husband or anyone else in the church anything you've told them.

    b. Not disclose to anyone where you are if you have gone somewhere safe.

3. Help you with spiritual issues:

    a. Pray with you and for you.

    b. Help you with any questions you have about the Bible and what God thinks about your situation.

    c. Offer to help you find a woman to mentor you through the next difficult period of your life.

4. Help you with practical issues:

    a. Refer you to local agencies that can help, such as women's crisis centers, legal services, counselors, child protection services, etc.

    b. Offer to help in the short term with any financial needs you may have.

For your husband, they would hopefully meet with him in a public place with two or three leaders from the church who are able to keep a confidence. This is to protect their physical safety as well as the confidentiality of your husband. At this meeting they would:

1. Not disclose anything you have said to them, nor would they confront him.

2. Be prepared for him to confront them, and/or for him to claim to have recently converted to Christianity.

3. Focus on how your husband perceives his relationship with you, and remind him of his obligations to provide a safe, loving home for his family.

4. Challenge any rationalizations he might give for his abusive behaviors, such as "Yeah, I am a little harsh, but she . . ." or "The Bible says the man is the head of the wife."

5. Help him distinguish between his feelings and his behaviors. Feeling angry and raging at someone are very different; harm comes when emotions are inappropriately expressed.

Tips from an Expert

When abusers kill themselves, they often kill their partners first.

6. Help him redefine masculine thinking. Show him "real men" don't need to use power and control over their wives.

7. Refer him to a batterer intervention program. Let him know they think this is his best chance to save his marriage.

8. Let him know they will be following up with him over the next several weeks/months.

9. Tell you immediately if he threatens to kill you or himself, and call the police.

10. Pray with him and for him.

Often a pastor or elder will want to try to single-handedly counsel an abusive man. Sgt. Stewart does not recommend doing this.[53] He explains the issues which cause a man to abuse his wife are very complicated, and require more time and skill to work through than a pastor has. For this reason, your husband would be better served by entering a treatment program for domestic violence offenders which is designed to deal with these issues. The program will need to last a year or longer for it to be effective.

Remember you should never enter into joint counseling with an abuser.[54]

Should My Husband Step Down from His Leadership Positions and Leave the Church?

At this point, you might feel your husband should be asked to step down from any leadership or teaching positions he may have in the church. After all, the apostle Paul says in Ephesians 5:11–13:

> *Have nothing to do with the fruitless deeds of darkness,*
>
> *but rather expose them. For it is shameful*
>
> *even to mention what the disobedient do in secret.*
>
> *But everything exposed by the light becomes visible.*

On page eight of her book *Battered but Not Broken*, Patricia Riddle Gaddis, a domestic violence shelter director, writes, "When abusers are allowed to hold leadership roles within the church, violence is in effect upheld as an acceptable Christian practice. Jesus said to the church in Laodicea in Revelation 3:15–16:

> *I know your deeds, that you are*
>
> *neither cold nor hot. I wish you*
>
> *were either one or the other! So,*
>
> *because you are lukewarm—*
>
> *neither hot nor cold—I am about*
>
> *to spit you out of my mouth."*

Tips *from an Expert*

The average faith leader receives three or less hours of domestic violence training while in seminary. For this reason, if your husband is willing to change, he should seek out a treatment program for domestic violence offenders.

Ms. Gaddis believes a church taking a lukewarm position on the issue of domestic violence weakens a congregation. No matter how prosperous a church may appear, if the pastor and leaders tolerate spouse abuse, they will not be able to go forward spiritually and experience the full blessings of God.

In addition, you may want your husband to leave the church so you and your children can attend in peace. Ms. Gaddis agrees with this. She says on page fifty-nine, "I believe telling the abuser to leave the congregation and to worship elsewhere is the only spiritually and scripturally correct thing to do. It shows batterers violence will not be tolerated by the faith community—and allows battered women and their children to worship in peace and regain their trust in a loving God."

Enforcing this for you will require some strong men from your church. In his book *Refuge* Sergeant Stewart says his biggest complaint with Christian men is that many of them are more concerned with being liked than with being right.[55] If men in the church *were* willing to step up and do what is right, women would have hope, and at times, even hope for the relationship.

If you are concerned for your safety, you may need to consider seeking a restraining order (see Chapter 28). Make sure your church has, or is willing to create, a policy for handling stalkers. If not, you and your children, and other church members, will not be safe if your husband decides to ignore the restraining order and show up at the church.

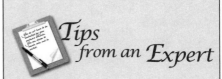

If you feel you need a restraining order, make sure your church has a policy for handling stalkers. If they don't, you, your children, and other church members will not be safe if your husband shows up at the church.

Sgt. Stewart gives an example in his book about a time when an abuser sat in church glaring at his wife during a service after she finally took her children to a women's shelter. The sergeant and a football player went to him on two different Sundays, telling him to leave. When the abuser realized men in the church were not afraid of him and were committed to doing the right thing for his wife, he decided to get the counseling he needed, and his marriage was saved.[56]

Just because your husband is not coming to Sunday morning services does not mean your pastors or elders should stop talking to him and holding him accountable. If he is willing to work with them, they can continue to keep in touch with him as he makes the changes in his life necessary for saving your relationship. Your pastor could also recommend another church for your husband to attend. This could be a friend's church. This pastor could then come alongside your husband as he takes the steps to make changes in his life.

Should I Consider Any Safety Issues?

Women's crisis centers often recommend an abuser *not* be asked to step down from leadership positions, or leave the church. They say the more losses an abusive man feels, the angrier he tends to become. For example, if he loses his position in the church, and is asked to leave the church altogether, he has lost two very important things. If this man has a tendency toward violence, this could send him over the edge. Churches meet at the same time every week. If your angry, abusive husband knows where you are every Sunday morning, he can find you easily, or wait for you in the parking lot—prepared to cause you or someone in your church harm.

You are the best judge of your safety. If you feel removing your husband from his positions or from the church altogether would put you in danger, you should ask your pastor and elders not to do this. If, on the other hand, you feel your husband would step down from his positions and leave the church quietly, then you could ask your church for this.

If you are afraid for your safety at any point during this process, you might decide to go to another church, at least for a time. This is your decision. If your pastor knows where you are going, make sure he promises to keep your whereabouts secret. Also, if you are afraid for your safety, you may want to seek a restraining order.

Debbie's Experience

Debbie's experience seeking help from the church was a bit unique because she was married to the pastor of her church. Her husband was having an affair with their sixteen-year-old babysitter, a member of their church. He would berate Debbie for long periods of time, then go out with the babysitter, leaving Debbie alone in her bedroom with a loaded Magnum .357 on her pillow, hoping she would take her own life. Debbie says she thought about using the gun, but held off for fear of what would happen to her three young children. She finally overcame her fear of her husband and told her sister, who lived in another state, what was happening. Her sister told Debbie if she didn't get some help, then she would expose her brother-in-law; calling every pastor in the city until Debbie got the help she needed.

So, Debbie called the wife of her denomination's state superintendent. Debbie asked her, "Where do you go when you're in the ministry, and your marriage is in trouble?" The superintendent's wife recommended a counseling program for Christians in the area. At the threat of being exposed by her sister, Debbie called the program, and made an appointment for the next day.

Like many abusers, Debbie's husband used finances to keep control over her; Debbie had no car or money of her own. So she took a bit of her very limited grocery money, put a small amount of gas into the church van, and drove herself to the counseling appointment.

When she told the counselor what was happening, he told her he wanted her to check into a hospital for a few days for some tests. He wrote a note, and told her to give it to her husband, which she did without reading it. Her husband called the counselor, who apparently threatened him, because the next morning he loaded Debbie and their three children into the car, and drove her to the hospital.

Not until she was given a form to fill out did Debbie realize she was being checked into the psychiatric ward of the hospital. She was so shocked she went numb. Her husband and children walked her down the hall, and then she had to wave good-bye to her children—one of the hardest things she had to do in her life.

During a counseling session, one of the nurses asked her, "Do you know how sick you are? You are telling us some of the most horrific things we have ever heard, and you are sitting there smiling." Debbie realized she had become the "perfect" pastor's wife—someone who denied her own feelings, and put everyone else first.

The hospital asked her husband to come in for counseling, but he refused. In the meantime, he told everyone in their church her mind had snapped, she was in the psychiatric hospital, and she had made up stories about him that weren't true. Because of this, the people in her church didn't know who to believe, or what to think.

However, other Christians rallied around Debbie. The denomination had a benevolence fund, which paid for Debbie's hospitalization and her and her children's counseling. The denomination's state superintendent and his wife, as well as people from other churches, bought her some nice clothes (she had very few). They also helped her with her self-esteem, which led to her eventually filing for divorce. When she and her children moved out of the parsonage (driving an old hippie Volkswagen bus from her grandmother), churches in the community paid for her to move into her own small home.

They were very poor. Some mornings, food would appear on their porch. People from her new church slipped her twenty dollar bills. Churches gave them gifts for Christmas. Since Debbie hadn't been allowed to work in the last ten years, a man in the church taught her how to sell life insurance.

In the meantime, their denomination put her husband, the pastor, under a disciplinary watch. He responded by attempting to persuade the church to leave the denomination. Eventually, the denomination took him to court to take the church building and parsonage away from him.

Debbie believes if her family and her denomination had not stepped in to help her and her children, she, and possibly her children, would be dead today.

Laura's Experience

Another woman, named Laura, also had a good experience receiving help from her church. When she told her pastor her husband had been emotionally and physically abusing her, he outlined steps both of them should take, including meeting weekly with accountability partners from the church and getting individual counseling.

The church supported her in taking whatever legal steps she felt necessary to be safe, including getting a restraining order. The church provided supervisors so her husband could visit with the children at the church. They also arranged for Christian attorneys to conduct mediation, and friends in the church met other financial needs.

She followed through with the steps outlined for her. Her husband began following through with his steps, but within a few weeks stopped meeting with his accountability partners. He eventually left the church. However, she felt protected, cared for, and loved throughout the entire difficult process. Like Debbie, Laura credits the intervention of the church with saving her life and providing a supportive extended family for her children.

In Conclusion

Marriages that suffer with domestic violence usually did not get to that state overnight, nor will they be saved overnight. This will be a long process, and will require the patience of many: you, your husband, and your church. If your pastor and/or elders are willing to stick with you both over a long period of time, your marriage might be saved.

CHAPTER 21:

What Is a *Bad* Outcome of Telling the Church?

In the last Chapter, we looked at some examples of good outcomes when you bring your abuse problem to your church. I pray if you *do* go to your church for help with your problem, they will help you in the ways described.

Unfortunately, this is not often the case. In *Keeping the Faith: Guidance for Christian Woman Facing Abuse,* Marie M. Fortune writes, "If you found your pastor or priest unhelpful, if you were not believed, or you were counseled to:

- Submit to your husband
- Pray harder
- Try to get your husband to church
- Be a better Christian wife
- Lift up the abuse to the Lord
- Forgive your abuser and take him back

> *A pastor who counsels any of the following:*
>
> - Submit to your husband
> - Pray harder
> - Be a better wife
>
> *can't help you. Don't feel guilty about looking elsewhere for help.*

without dealing with the battering and abuse, then that person does not understand what you have been through. He or she has no comprehension of your experience and no information about wife abuse. At this point, this person will not be a helpful resource to you.[57]

"Remember most ministers have not received any training to prepare them for understanding your abuse. Although they may care deeply about you and want to help, their lack of knowledge and skill will prevent them from being the support you need. Do not feel guilty about choosing not to discuss your abuse further with your minister at this time. God will provide other pastors or priests, or godly lay people, who may be more knowl-edgeable and prepared to help."

My Experience with the Church

In Chapter 19, I described how I went to my church two different times for help. The first pastor I spoke with offered to pray for me, but did noth-ing else. A year and a half later, I spoke to a different pastor. This pastor of-fered to follow through with my husband. Unfortunately, my husband did not change his behavior when confronted by our pastor. In fact, his abuse escalated. He began doing things like waking me in the night to scream at me, and threatening to divorce me on an almost daily basis. One day he told me that in ten minutes he was going to tell our children we were getting a divorce (though he didn't follow through with the threat). He showed no sign of repentance. Everything that had happened was "my fault." Now he was going to "have to" leave the church because I had "hu-miliated" him publicly.

I had asked my pastor to call my husband and hold him accountable for his behavior. My pastor called my husband for a few weeks. My hus-band told him our relationship was getting better, though that was not the case. Our pastor also called me a few times, and I told him what was really happening. After a while, my husband told me to tell the pastor to stop talking to me. Out of fear of my husband, I did. Of course, my husband didn't want the pastor to talk to me! I was telling him the truth about what was happening in our home. I was secretly hoping the pastor would realize this was just one more way my husband was trying to control me. I was very disappointed in the pastor when he agreed not to call me anymore. From then on, I received no more support from the church.

My Experience with a Christian Counselor Who was Uneducated About Domestic Violence

During this same time period, my husband agreed to see a Christian counselor—as long as it was someone he chose. This counselor was, un-fortunately, not trained in domestic violence. When my husband initially went to him, he did not tell him the frightening and abusive things he was doing. When I finally asked to meet alone with the counselor, the counsel-or was very surprised at the things I told him. After the counselor outlined steps for me to take to create a safety plan, he suggested my husband and I meet with him together. (Remember, as I mentioned in Chapter 9, many states prohibit couples counseling for abusers.)

My experience with joint counseling confirms it is dangerous to allow couples to be counseled together when domestic violence is in the relationship. Meeting the counselor together with my husband did not help things at all. In fact, it made things much worse:

- During one counseling session, I said my childhood was pretty good. My husband became enraged! This was because he had been telling the counselor I was just misunderstanding his actions based on my childhood experiences.

- Our counselor suggested I tell my husband the actions he was doing that hurt me. This gave my husband even more ammunition to hurt me with. For example, when I told him when he didn't speak to me that it hurt me, he spoke to me even less, and began pretending I physically did not exist in our home.

After just a few weeks, the counselor realized meeting as a couple was not working, so he began seeing each of us individually. This was also not helpful because the counselor would tell my husband things I had told him in confidence.

Looking back, I think meeting with this counselor one time to explain what was really happening in our home was good for me, but then I should have let him and my husband work together without me. After that, I should have found a counselor of my own who was an expert in domestic violence.

After about six months of meeting with the counselor together and separately, the counselor told my husband and me how he felt he was not able to help us, and suggested we find another counselor. I was shocked and angry. At the end of the session, I asked to speak to the counselor alone, and he told me why he was recommending this. He said my husband had spent the last six private sessions yelling at the counselor. He was furious the counselor refused to tell me I had been wrong for going to the church for help.

I was so hurt. I had now gone to *three* Christian men seeking help: two pastors at my church at two different times, and a Christian counselor. They had all abandoned me in one way or another. I am thankful I had surrounded myself with supportive Christian women. They helped me keep my eyes on Jesus and strengthen my own walk with the Lord. They never abandoned me, and neither did my Savior. Through it all, I felt Jesus holding my hand.

I have spoken to other Christian women who were abused by their husbands. They had also turned to their church for help and, in one way or another, the church let them down. Because of this some of these women, for a time at least, stopped going to church completely. If Christians let you down during your time of need, I pray you will not stop attending church. Leave a specific church if that is what you feel God is leading you to do, but do not forsake the Lord or His body, the church, completely. You need the Lord and His people more now than ever.

If your church refuses to use the Matthew 18 process and hold your husband accountable, you may have to get the safety you need without their help. The important thing is you will have given the church a chance to do what it is meant to do. Like Debbie, you might receive help through your denomination or other churches in your area. Or, you might receive help from one or more Christian couples or women. Or you may receive help from others beyond your Christian community—such as domestic violence crisis centers, etc. However you receive the help, God will be by your side.

CHAPTER 22:

If God Hates Divorce, Can You Ever Leave Your Husband?

You may be asking yourself if leaving your abusive husband is OK in the eyes of the Lord. You may have read or been told, "God hates divorce." Let us look at this verse in context. Malachi 2:15–16 says:

> *Has not the LORD made them one? In flesh and spirit they are his. And why one? Because he was seeking godly offspring. So guard yourself in your spirit, and do not break faith with the wife of your youth. "I hate divorce," says the LORD God of Israel, "and I hate a man's covering himself with violence as well as with his garment," says the LORD Almighty.*

In this passage, Israelite men were divorcing the godly Israelite wives they had married in their youth, and were marrying instead the idol worshiping women of surrounding tribes. God was saying He hated what these men were doing. He hated that *these men* were *covering themselves* with *violence* (an excellent description of domestic violence). He also hated how they were leaving godly women who would produce godly offspring, and marrying idol worshipers, who would produce children who would worship idols instead of the one true God. Here are a few other versions of verse 16a:

> *'The man who hates and divorces his wife,' says the LORD, the God of Israel,*
> *'does violence to the one he should protect,' says the LORD Almighty*
> (NIV 2011)

> *'For the man who does not love his wife but divorces her, says the LORD, the God of Israel, covers his garment with violence, says the LORD of hosts.'*
> (ESV)

In these verses, the Lord is clearly putting the blame on the husband who hates his wife, and is committing violence against her.

Perhaps your abusive husband has used this or other Bible verses to make you believe you would be sinning if you left him. Many well-meaning pastors, elders, and other Christians might agree. They might say sexual unfaithfulness and abandonment by an unbelieving spouse are the only biblical grounds for divorce. The church has traditionally focused on Jesus's and Paul's words about divorce in the New Testament, and has completely ignored what the Old Testament has to say about divorce.

> *Jesus and Paul knew the Old Testament completely. Their comments about divorce were meant to add to, not replace or change, what was already written in the Old Testament about marriage and divorce.*

When I was trying to make the difficult decision whether to stay in my abusive marriage or leave it, I was not able to find many Christian resources. Not until after I asked for a legal separation did a friend put a little booklet into my hand called *God's Protection of Women: When Abuse is Worse than Divorce.* Herb Vander Lugt, author and senior research editor for RBC Ministries, a well-respected Christian ministry, wrote this booklet. To request it, go to www.rbc.net.

The unusual thing about this booklet is that it examines the entire Bible, both Old and New Testaments, to discern what God says about protecting a wife in an abusive marriage. Mr. Vander Lugt explains how Jesus and Paul both knew the Old Testament completely, and their comments were meant to add to, rather than replace or change, what was already said in the Old Testament about marriage and divorce. After all, Paul wrote to Timothy, in 2 Timothy 3:16–17:

> *All Scripture is God-breathed and is useful for teaching,*
>
> *rebuking, correcting, and training in righteousness, so that the*
>
> *man of God may be thoroughly equipped for every good work.*

In the following sections, I will summarize Mr. Vander Lugt's thoughts from *God's Protection of Women.*[58]

Old Testament Divorce Laws that Protected Women

In the days of Moses, women were regarded as property, to be used and traded in the same manner as an ox or a piece of land. Wives were expected to remain absolutely sexually faithful to their husbands, but no such demand was placed on husbands. In that time, fathers could sell their daughters to fellow Israelites to pay off financial debts (Exodus 21:7–11). In addition, when soldiers won a battle, they could force women captured as prisoners of war to become their wives (Deuteronomy 21:10–14). These circumstances seem abhorrent to us today, but were commonplace in Moses's time. In both these cases, God imposed limitations on these practices to soften their cruelty. In both, if the husband was not pleased with the woman for some reason (which is not specified), he was forced to let her "go free." He was prohibited from using her as a common slave, from selling her to someone else, and from treating her brutally. He could not diminish her clothing, her food, or her marriage rights (probably referring to her right to bear children). The expression "go free"[59] means the law required the husband to give her a certificate of divorce, whether or not he wanted to.

Those laws discussed divorce for slave women in Israel. Divorce for free Israelite women is discussed by Moses in Deuteronomy 24:1–4:

> *If a man marries a woman who becomes displeasing to him*
> *because he finds something indecent about her, and he writes*
> *her a certificate of divorce, gives it to her and sends her from his*
> *house, and if after she leaves his house she becomes the wife of*
> *another man, and her second husband dislikes her and writes*
> *her a certificate of divorce, gives it to her and sends her from his*
> *house, or if he dies, then her first husband, who divorced her, is*
> *not allowed to marry her again after she has been defiled. That*
> *would be detestable in the eyes of the LORD. Do not bring sin upon*
> *the land the LORD your God is giving you as an inheritance.*

In this passage, no specific reason is given for the man giving her a certificate of divorce, and she is clearly allowed to remarry afterward. The only restriction seems to be that they are not allowed to remarry each other if she has been married to someone else in the meantime. Why would this be? One possibility is that this might discourage a casual attitude toward divorce and remarriage.

A Time in the Old Testament When God Encouraged His People to Divorce

Though God hates divorce, at times He has felt it was necessary, as shown in Ezra chapters 9 and 10.

In these chapters, the people came to Ezra and confessed they had married wives from the idol worshiping peoples who surrounded them. Ezra was appalled. After "praying and confessing, weeping and throwing himself down before the house of God," (Ezra 10:1) the people came to him, and they covenanted before God to send away all the foreign wives and their children. Ezra agreed, and made a proclamation, saying, "You have been unfaithful; you have married foreign women, adding to Israel's guilt. Now make confession to the LORD, the God of your fathers, and do his will. Separate yourselves from the peoples around you and from your foreign wives." (Ezra 10:10b–11)

What Does Jesus Say in the New Testament?

Many Christians will say only two reasons are valid for divorce in the Bible: sexual unfaithfulness (according to Jesus), and being abandoned by an unbeliever (according to the apostle Paul). Let's examine these claims further.

In the Sermon on the Mount (Matthew 5), Jesus is focusing His listeners on the deep issues of the soul. He points out the damage self-righteous husbands were doing to their wives when they divorced them for something other than sexual unfaithfulness (Matthew 5:31–32). According to Dr. Dallas Willard, professor at USC, speaker, and author, a divorced woman in Jesus's time had three choices. She could:

1. Become a burden to a generous relative—usually as no more than a servant,

2. Become a wife to another man as "damaged goods," or

3. Become a prostitute.[60]

Jesus knew all the Old Testament laws. A few verses earlier, in Matthew 5:17–20, He had just said He had not come to get rid of the Old Testament law, but to fulfill it. In verses 5:31–32, He was not giving a full treatise on divorce law. Looking at the context, Jesus possibly was confronting the self-righteousness of hard-hearted men. He was focusing on men who were "adulterizing" their wives by causing them and those who married them to live in a state that falls short of God's original intent for marriage.

Similarly, in Matthew 19:1–9, Jesus is not responding to an abused woman, but to self-righteous Pharisees who are trying to pit Jesus's words against those of Moses. Vander Lugt believes Jesus was giving insight, rather than legislation. He was not giving the full answer about divorce here anymore than He was giving the full answer about how one could have eternal life a few verses later, when speaking to the young man (Matthew 19:16–20).[61] Jesus points the Pharisees back to God's original design for marriage as a teacher of righteousness. He tells them how Moses allowed them to divorce because their "hearts were hard," (for our purposes a good description of an abusive man who refuses to change).

Dr. Willard says:

"No doubt what was foremost in Jesus' mind was the fact the woman could quite well wind up dead, or brutally abused, if the man could not 'dump' her. Better then that divorce occurs than life be made unbearable. We must resist any attempt to classify divorce as a special, irredeemable form of wickedness. It is not. It is sometimes the right thing to do, everything considered."[62]

What Does the Apostle Paul Say?

Some Christians believe the apostle Paul says abandonment by an unbeliever is the only acceptable reason for divorce (1 Corinthians 7:1–16). Given Paul was a Pharisee, he knew the Mosaic Law backward and forward, and given he was the most ardent follower of Jesus, him discounting anything Moses had written about divorce, or anything Jesus had said about it, is highly unlikely. Vander Lugt, therefore, surmises that Paul is building his comments about divorce *onto* those of Moses and Jesus, rather than *in place* of them. He believes this because chapter 7 of 1 Corinthians begins by saying, "Now for the matters you wrote about," thus Paul was writing to answer questions raised by the believers in Corinth.[63]

Corinth in Paul's time was a city marked by great sexual immorality. Some of the believers apparently thought the most complete way of expressing their devotion to Christ was sexual abstinence, even within marriage. Paul says he wishes others were like him, and could give single-minded devotion to Christ without being overwhelmed by sexual temptation, but he realized this was not the case. In this immediate context, Paul urges wives not to divorce their husbands, and if they did leave, to remain unmarried or be reconciled. He then goes on to address a situation that had not been discussed in the Scriptures before—a believing wife or husband living with an unbelieving spouse. He completes this section by saying, "God has called us to live in peace." Clearly, he recognizes the intent of the marriage covenant.

What Have We Seen so Far?

We see the Bible has a lot to say about divorce. Let's recap what we've seen so far:

1. In the Old Testament, Moses set out laws to protect the weakest women in society, women sold as slaves, and foreign women taken as captives to be made wives. Though such a woman was considered a piece of property, and could not ask for a divorce herself, if her husband didn't treat her well, her husband had to grant her a certificate of divorce.

2. Women who were granted a certificate of divorce were allowed to marry another; the only condition was they could not remarry their first husband if they had married someone else in the meantime.

3. God said He hated the *specific* divorces in Malachi 2, where the Israelite men were divorcing their Israelite women to marry idol worshiping wives. He said He hated "a man who covers himself in violence."

4. Though God hates divorce, He required the Israelite men to divorce their pagan, idol worshiping wives in order not to defile the people of Israel.

5. Jesus, knowing all the laws set out by Moses, and while speaking to self-righteous Pharisees, says the only reason *they* can divorce their wives is for marital unfaithfulness, in the same chapter where He tells the young ruler the way to eternal life is to sell all his possessions and follow Him.

6. Paul, knowing all the laws set out by Moses, and what Jesus had

already said about divorce, answers questions asked by the Corinthians about sexual abstinence, and how it pertains to marriage.

Perhaps, after looking at all the Scriptures above, you or someone in your church is still struggling with whether the Bible gives you permission to leave your abusive husband. If so, we should consider that Jesus showed how He is more concerned with the people and the *intent* of the law than He is about the *letter* of the law. He was often angry with those who put more value on keeping the Sabbath law than on showing love toward those the law was meant to protect. In Luke 13:10–17, Jesus heals a woman who had been crippled for eighteen years on the Sabbath. The synagogue ruler becomes indignant that Jesus healed the woman on the Sabbath. Jesus calls the man a hypocrite, saying in verses 15 and 16:

> *"Doesn't each of you on the Sabbath untie his ox or donkey*
> *from the stall and lead it out to give it water?*
> *Then should not this woman, a daughter of Abraham, whom*
> *Satan has kept bound for eighteen long years,*
> *be set free on the Sabbath day from what bound her?"*

Seeing the connection between this woman's situation and yours can be difficult, can't it? You are also a daughter of Abraham, and you have been bound by someone's ungodly actions. Shouldn't you be set free from what is binding you, rather than be held captive by someone else's interpretation of a verse in the Bible?

In another instance, in Mark 2:23–27, we find Jesus and His disciples walking through a field on the Sabbath. The disciples are hungry, and they pull off some pieces of grain to eat as they walk. When the Pharisees complain about this, Jesus reminds them of the time when King David and his companions were hungry, and went into the house

> *Jesus is more concerned with people and the **intent** of the law than He is about the **letter** of the law. He was often angered by those who put more value on keeping Sabbath law than on showing love for those the law was meant to protect.*

of God and ate the consecrated bread. Jesus concludes by saying in verse 27:

"The Sabbath was made for man, not man for the Sabbath."

In a similar way, we can say marriage was made for men and women, not that men and women were made for marriage.

In Conclusion

In the conclusion to the booklet *God's Protection of Women,* Vander Lugt writes, "May our Lord help us to know when to work hard for reconciliation, and when to be willing to grieve with those who are experiencing the pain of lost dreams and broken promises."[64]

Constructive Desertion

In his book *A Cry for Justice: How the Evil of Domestic Abuse Hides in Your Church,* Pastor Jeff Crippen, an evangelical pastor, has also studied what the Bible says about divorce.[65]

Crippen says a husband's being "willing to live" with his wife means showing "understanding and deference" to her.

When looking at 1 Corinthians 7:13, which says:

And if a woman has a husband who is not a believer and he is

willing to live with her, she must not

divorce him.

Crippen says the phrase willing to live with her "cannot be limited to a narrow, wooden definition such as 'if the unbeliever agrees to remain in the same house with the Christian'. As Peter seems to indicate in his use of a very similar Greek word, 'to live with' means to 'remain in the marriage, showing understanding and deference to one's spouse.'"[66] As we see in 1 Peter 3:7:

*Crippen calls domestic abuse "constructive desertion," because the abuser's evil conduct causes the victim to leave. In this case, the **abuser** is the deserter, **not the victim.***

Husbands, in the same way be considerate as you live with your wives,

and treat them with respect as the weaker partner and as heirs with

you of the gracious gift of life, so that nothing will hinder your prayers.

Crippen contends that domestic abuse is a form of desertion, calling it "constructive desertion." He says, "'Constructive desertion' occurs when one partner's evil conduct ends the marriage because it causes the other partner to leave. *But the <u>abuser</u> is to be construed as the deserter, not the victim. The victim bears no blame.*"[67]

Marriage as a Contract

Crippen looks at marriage as a contract, just like any other contract we enter into.[68] In a contract, each party makes promises. Blessings are given if both parties keep their promises, and curses are given if one of the parties doesn't. For example, I promise to pay my mortgage to the bank, and they promise to allow me to continue living in my home. If I pay my mortgage on time, I have the *blessing* of being allowed to continue living in my house. If I refuse to pay my mortgage, *curses* go into effect. They can evict me from my house!

When spouses enter into a marriage contract, they make promises to each other before witnesses, and *before God*. Spouses usually promise to:

- Love
- Honor
- Cherish
- Forsake all others
- Until death

In abusive marriages, the abuser breaks these promises daily. But unlike every other contract, the Christian victim appears to have no recourse. She is told she cannot break her part of the contract even though the other party (the abusive spouse) never loves, honors, or cherishes her. He receives no *curses* for breaking his part of the contract, but continues to receive all the *blessings* forever. As Crippen says, "Something is really wrong with this picture!"[69]

Divorce has two parts:

1. Destruction of the marriage—caused by habitual breaking of vows by the abuser.

2. Divorce of the marriage—when the marriage is over, the innocent victim may, without sin, file for divorce with civil authorities.

Crippen says divorce has two parts:

1. **Destruction of the marriage**—accomplished by the willful, habitual, unrepentant breaking of the vows by the abuser. This is what causes the marriage to end.

2. **Divorce of the marriage**—when the marriage is over, the innocent victim may then, without sin, file for divorce from the civil authorities.

In Matthew 19:6b Jesus says,

Therefore what God has joined together, let man not separate.

Crippen concludes, "But Jesus did not teach the human marriage covenant is impossible to break. In fact, he instructed no one *should* break it, indicating that by violation of the vows . . . the guilty spouse separates what God has joined together. Separating what God has joined together is *always* sin, but only for the guilty spouse."[70]

CHAPTER 23:

How Do You Face Your Church Friends If You Leave Him?

One thing holding you back from taking steps to leave your abusive husband may be fear of what your friends, family, or fellow church members will say or think. I really struggled with this. Finally, my counselor at the women's crisis center asked me, "If the people who know you well knew what was happening in your home, would they really think badly of you for leaving?" The answer was definitely no. This helped me put my fears to rest.

I have a friend who was not so fortunate. She received harassing phone calls from her prayer and Bible study groups telling her she would burn in Hell if she divorced and how she just needed to take the abuse because that was God's will. I pray this won't happen to you. If it does, you will need to *stand firm* (Ephesians 6:14) in the Lord, and lean on the support system you have created. In this Chapter, I will help you think through some statements people might say to you.

1. "You should never give up."[71]
   This sounds good, and even biblical. It sounds like you should always have hope in the Lord. If you believe this, you may think leaving your abusive husband means you have failed in some way. However, Proverbs 27:12 says:

   > A prudent man sees danger and takes refuge,
   >
   > but the simple keep going and suffer for it.

   A time comes when you have done everything in your power to save your marriage. To stay longer puts you in more danger.

2. "Sticks and stones may break your bones, but words will never hurt you," or "His bark is worse than his bite," or "People don't always mean what they say," or "You can rise above it."[72]

If you believe these statements, you may think that no matter what he says you shouldn't feel hurt, no matter how badly you feel. This is simply not true. Many women who were physically abused say the emotional abuse they experienced took longer to recover from than the physical abuse. David says in Psalm 55:12–14:

> *If an enemy were insulting me,*
>
> *I could endure it;*
>
> *if a foe were raising himself against me,*
>
> *I could hide from him.*
>
> *But it is you, a man like myself,*
>
> *my companion, my close friend,*
>
> *with whom I once enjoyed sweet fellowship*

3. "Christians should never judge each other."
   Webster's Dictionary defines the verb judge in two ways:
   a. To sit in judgment on.
   b. To form an opinion about through careful weighing of evidence and testing of premises.

   In other words, we have two types of judgment. The first definition implies criticism and condemnation of a person. Jesus is referring to this definition when he tells us not to judge others in Matthew 7:1–2:

> *"Do not judge, or you too will be judged.*
>
> *For in the same way you judge others,*
>
> *you will be judged, and with the measure you use,*
>
> *it will be measured to you.*

Because we are taught as Christians to not be judgmental of another person, you may have difficulty discerning whether your husband is abusive. This is why I encouraged you in Chapter 4 to take a hard look at your own behavior. No Christian wants to be in the position of condemning another Christian for behavior we ourselves are doing.

However, the other type of judgment Jesus *does* promote—analyzing and evaluating a person's actions.

Jesus says in Matthew 7:15:

Watch out for false prophets. They come to you in sheep's clothing, but inwardly they are ferocious wolves.

Then, in verses 20–21:

Thus, by their fruit you will recognize them. "Not everyone who says to me, 'Lord, Lord,' will enter the kingdom of heaven, but only he who does the will of my Father who is in heaven.

Finally, in verse 23:

Then I will tell them plainly, 'I never knew you. Away from me, you evildoers!'

In this passage, Jesus is *telling* us to judge by "forming an opinion" about people claiming to be prophets. He says that "by their fruit you will recognize them," implying we should look at the fruit in a person's life to discern if they truly can be prophets.

Paul also encourages believers to use discernment when dealing with brothers in the church. In 1 Corinthians 5:1–8 he chastises the Corinthian church for allowing a man who is sleeping with his father's wife to remain in the congregation. Paul says he has:

... already passed judgment on the one who did this, just as if I were present.

(1 Corinthians 5:3)

> *We are taught not to judge others by condemning them. However, both Jesus and Paul encouraged believers to use discernment when evaluating a "believer's" actions.*

In other words, Paul is saying Christians can judge whether a person should be allowed in their congregation based upon that person's behavior. So, in summary, we are taught to not judge a brother in the sense of condemning him, but we are required to be discerning about a person's sinful behavior.

4. "God hates divorce."
   The implication is that since God hates it, seeking it is wrong. This saying is taken from Malachi 2:15–16. The context of this passage is that Israelite men were divorcing their Hebrew wives so they could marry pagan wives. The wording of these verses reads:

   Has not the Lord made them one?

   In flesh and spirit they are his. And why one?

   Because he was seeking godly offspring.

   So guard yourself in your spirit,

   and do not break faith with the wife of your youth.

   "I hate divorce," says the Lord God of Israel,

   "and I hate a man's covering himself with violence

   as well as with his garment," says the Lord Almighty.

   I love these verses. What the Lord hates is a man covering himself in violence, and a man breaking faith with the wife of his youth. This truly describes an emotional or physical abuser. The Lord places the blame for the end of the marriage with the man who covers himself with violence.

5. "A Christian should not take another Christian to court."
   This statement is taken from Paul's exhortation to the Corinthian church in 1 Corinthians 6:1–2:

   If any of you has a dispute with another,

   dare he take it before the ungodly for judgment

   instead of before the saints?

   Do you not know that the saints will judge the world?

   And if you are to judge the world,

   are you not competent to judge trivial cases?

   And in verse 7:

   The very fact that you have lawsuits among you

   means you have been completely defeated already.

Why not rather be wronged?

Why not rather be cheated?

The NIV study Bible's footnotes on this passage say: "Paul seems to be talking about various kinds of property court cases here (see the phrase 'rather be cheated,' vs. 7), not criminal cases that should be handled by the state (see Romans 13:3–4)."

Romans 13:3–4 says:

For rulers hold no terror for those who do right,

but for those who do wrong.

Do you want to be free from fear of the one in authority?

Then do what is right and he will commend you.

For he is God's servant to do you good.

But if you do wrong, be afraid,

for he does not bear the sword for nothing.

He is God's servant, an agent of wrath

to bring punishment on the wrongdoer.

If you have already turned to your church seeking help, then you have already sought the help of the brothers. If your husband continues behaving abusively after you have taken all the steps I mentioned in Chapters 18 through 21, you may then, without guilt, seek help from the government God has established. As it says in Romans 13:1:

Everyone must submit himself to the governing authorities,

for there is no authority except

that which God has established.

The authorities that exist have been established by God.

In addition, if you have gone through the Matthew 18 process, and your husband has refused to change his behavior, the church would treat him as an unbeliever. As it says in Matthew 18:17:

If he refuses to listen, tell it to the church;

and if he refuses to listen even to the church,

treat him as you would a pagan or a tax collector.

In this case, you are no longer taking a believer to court.

I hope this Chapter has helped you think through some of the objections Christians might have about you leaving your abusive husband who refuses to change his behavior. This is a difficult decision. No one can make it for you, or rush you into it.

CHAPTER 24:

What if You Still Have Questions in Your Heart?

In Chapter 22, we saw Herb Vander Lugt's and Jeff Crippen's arguments that the Bible gives permission for a woman to leave her abusive husband. In Chapter 23, we countered objections other Christians might have. However, you may still have some doubts in your own heart. I can't possibly anticipate every question you might struggle with. However, I will try to address some key questions in this Chapter.

Some Common Questions Women Ask Themselves

In her book *Keeping the Faith: Guidance for Christian Women Facing Abuse*, Marie Fortune, a minister and director of the Center for Prevention of Sexual and Domestic Violence in Seattle, discusses these common questions:[73]

1. *"He needs me now more than ever. How can he change without me to help him? Shouldn't I stay and take care of him?"*

Ms. Fortune answers, "As long as you are with him, you are an occasion for his sin. In other words, you are the one whom he feels safe abusing, and as long as you are there, he will abuse you; he will continue with his sinful behavior. This does not mean you are responsible for his behavior; it is not your fault."

> *Your husband's best hope for change is a treatment program for abusers. If you leave him, even temporarily, he may get the message you will no longer tolerate his abuse.*

Your husband's best hope for change is to work with a treatment program for abusers. If you leave him, even temporarily, he may get the message you will no longer tolerate his abuse.

2. *"I would like to talk with someone about my situation and maybe go somewhere safe for a while. But, I don't think those people at the shelter are Christians. I'm afraid they may try to take away my faith."*

Ms. Fortune answers, "When your house is on fire, and you call the firefighters to come put out the fire, do you stop and ask those people whether or not they are Christians?"

I (Caroline) sought help from the National Domestic Violence Hotline and my local women's crisis center, neither of which is specifically Christian. They obviously worked with Christian women who had questions about what God thought about leaving their abusive husbands. They were sensitive and kind, and did *not* try to talk me out of my faith.

3. *"I don't want to go to that shelter. No one like me will be there."*

Ms. Fortune responds, "You may be right; you may not meet anyone like you, but you may be surprised, too. Women of all ages, races, religious groups, and family styles are abused and go to crisis centers or safe homes."

4. *"If I leave him, I don't know how I will take care of myself and the kids. I don't have a job right now. How will I pay the bills or rent an apartment?"*

Many abused women feel this way. You may also feel frightened about living on your own, making all the decisions yourself, or simply be afraid of change. No one would try to tell you this would be easy. Keep in mind what Proverbs 15:17 says, "Better a meal of vegetables where there is love than a fattened calf with hatred."

Also, be assured Jesus will walk with you every step of the way. As He says in Matthew 6:25–27:

> *Therefore I tell you, do not worry about your life,*
>
> *what you will eat or drink; or about your body,*
>
> *what you will wear. Is not life more important than food,*
>
> *and the body more important than clothes?*
>
> *Look at the birds of the air;*
>
> *they do not sow or reap or store away in barns,*
>
> *and yet your heavenly Father feeds them.*
>
> *Are you not much more valuable than they?*
>
> *Who of you by worrying can add a single hour to his life?*

Jesus can guide you to the help you need. Do not be afraid to lean on Him and His people. You can turn to family, friends, and your church. In addition, your local women's crisis center will be able to connect you with many resources in your community. This is a time when you can put your full trust in Jesus, possibly for the first time in your life. This may turn out to be a great time of growth in your faith as He fulfills your needs day by day. Psalm 9:9-10 says:

> *Being afraid of living alone is natural. Now is a time to lean on others and the Lord. This can be a time of great spiritual growth.*

> *The LORD is a refuge for the oppressed,*
>
> *a stronghold in times of trouble.*
>
> *Those who know your name will trust in you,*
>
> *for you, LORD, have never forsaken those who seek you.*

He's Threatened to Take Away My Children, Now What?

5. *"I'm afraid of losing my children. My husband sometimes threatens to kidnap them, and the next day tells me he will petition for full custody. I'm sure he could do either."*

Fear of losing their children is probably one of the greatest reasons women stay in abusive relationships. Let's take these threats one at a time:

a) **Kidnapping**—while some men will kidnap their children, this is a fairly rare occurrence. If your husband did do this after you got some kind of legal help and left with them, he would have to leave his home, his job, his family, and probably the state. He would become a fugitive and, if caught, would go to jail. Most often, this is an idle threat coming from a bully, which is in essence what an abusive man is. When I left my abuser, thinking of him as a bully helped. Most schoolyard bullies make more threats than they actually carry out. Of course, this is not always the case. You know your husband best, and need to go with your gut regarding your own safety and the safety of your children.

b) **Full custody**—your husband may very well petition for full custody of your children. This is why preparing *before* you leave is very important, if that is at all possible. We will talk about preparation in Chapter 26. Perhaps the thought of your husband having *any* custody of your children without your protection gives you chills. Unfortunately, chances are good he will get *some* custody (or parenting time) with them, no matter what kind of proof of abuse you have. Keep in mind that right now, he is with them *all the time*, and in reality, you are not able to protect them *at all.* If they are with you part of the time, they will be able to see the difference between how you behave and how he does. They will know that by leaving you have shown them his abuse was not acceptable. This will make a big impact on them in the long run.

What Do I Do If He's Threatened Me?

6. *"I'm afraid if I leave my husband will physically hurt me. He has made all kinds of threats. He has even threatened to kill me if I ever leave him."*

This is one of the greatest fears abused women have, and is a very real fear. The most dangerous time for an abused woman is when she leaves her abuser—a proven fact. This is why you must do your safety planning, whether you plan to leave or plan to stay. Get the help of others, such as your local women's crisis center. They can help you discern whether leaving is your safest option, and they can help you with things such as getting a restraining (or protection) order. They can also help you find a safe place to go.

Is Staying *Ever* Safe?

7. *"Is staying ever safe?"*

While leaving the relationship is usually safer, some women stay because they feel that is the safer choice for them. I have spoken to domestic violence advocates who say women come and stay at their shelter temporarily whenever their husbands are in the explosive stage of the abuse cycle. Then, when he moves into the honeymoon stage, they return home. Since this book is mainly addressing emotional and spiritual abuse, I personally think permanently leaving the situation *before* it becomes physically violent is better. Also, remember these types of abuse can be more damaging to the victim's heart, mind, and soul than physical abuse. However, each woman must decide the best choice for her long-term safety and that of her children and pets.

1. Would you feel comfortable seeking help from someone at your church? Why or why not?

2. Would you want your husband to leave the church and/or step down from any leadership positions he might have in the church?

A Drink of Water for the Journey

"The day we find the perfect church, it becomes imperfect the moment we join it."

Charles Spurgeon

3. If your church was unhelpful, or let you down when you asked for help, would you feel let down by God? Would you seek a new church?

4. Having read the Bible verses presented in Chapter 22, do you believe the Bible gives women freedom to divorce their abusive husbands?

5. Have you ever heard any of the statements made in Chapter 23 about why a woman should not leave her abusive husband? If so, which ones? What do you think about these statements after reading Chapter 23?

6. Which questions in Chapter 24 did you most identify with? Do you feel better about any concerns you may have after reading the explanations given in the Chapter?

SECTION 7:

Making the Decision to Leave or Stay

CHAPTER 25:

Has the Time Come to Leave?

If you are at this point in the process, you have hopefully:

1. Examined your own behavior and motives in your relationship, and changed any behaviors of yours you believe are displeasing to the Lord.

2. You are aware of a continuing pattern of abuse in your relationship, and you have examined your values and beliefs about the impact of the abuse on you and your children.

3. You have educated yourself about domestic violence via books, the Internet, counselors, and support groups.

4. You have acquired a support system of friends who will pray for you and support your safety.

5. You have spent quite a bit of time standing firm and setting boundaries against the abuse to let your husband know you will no longer accept abuse from him.

6. You have asked two appropriate men to confront your husband and hold him accountable for changing his behavior, as Jesus instructs us in Matthew 18:16.

7. You have brought your problem to the church, and asked for their help, *or* you have decided your church is not a safe place for you to receive the help you need.

8. You have searched the Scriptures and considered what the Bible says about leaving an abusive husband whose heart is hard, and who refuses to change.

9. You have searched your heart, prayed, and asked God what His will for you is.

If you see no real change in your husband's behavior after going through all of the steps outlined above, has the time come for you to separate from your husband?

Are You Afraid of Your Husband?

The first question to ask yourself is: are you afraid of your husband? You don't need to overanalyze this question. If your heart pounds each time you hear his footsteps approaching, you are afraid of him. If you feel you need to hide your thoughts and actions from him most of the time, you are afraid of him.

Where Would the Children *Really* be Better Off?

If you have children, the second question you should ask yourself is if the children are *really* better off if the marriage stays intact? Consider the example you and your husband are setting. Are you teaching your children treating women with disrespect is OK, or accepting disrespect is OK? Are they learning God designed marriage to be filled with hatred and fear?

Often an abused woman who has children will be tempted to wait it out until her children are grown, but that may be too late for her, *and* for her children. She may become severely crippled physically, emotionally, and/or spiritually, or even killed by then. And, her children will probably become targets of the violence. In her book *Battered but Not Broken*, Ms. Gaddis says, "Seventy percent of men who abuse their

> "Seventy percent of men who abuse their wives also abuse their children . . .
>
> the symptoms are cyclical: up to 70 percent of men who abuse their wives grew up witnessing their fathers abuse their mothers. Children who live in violent homes come to accept this as a way of life—and pass it on."

wives also abuse their children . . . the symptoms are cyclical: up to 70 percent of men who abuse their wives grew up witnessing their fathers abuse their mothers. Children who live in violent homes come to accept this as a way of life—and pass it on."[74]

I was concerned what my husband's behavior was teaching my daughters about what they should look for and accept from a potential mate. I was even more concerned about how my sons would treat their future wives. In fact, this question led me to eventually separate from my husband. I decided after many years of escalating abuse that my children living under the leadership of an abusive father was worse than separating from my husband.

Has the Time Come to Leave?

So, we are back to the question asked at the beginning of this Chapter. As a Christian woman in an abusive relationship, do you and your children stay with your abusive husband, or do you leave him, at least for a time? This is probably one of the hardest decisions you will ever have to make. Unfortunately, no one else can make this decision for you. Well-meaning friends and family may *think* they know what is best for you. They may be sure you should leave immediately, or they may feel you should "honor your marriage vows," and stay. What they think does not matter. Bring this decision to the Lord, and He will help you decide what is best. Spend time with Him in prayer, and ask Him to help you discern His will for you. He will help you feel at peace with your decision. Colossians 3:15 (NLT) says:

And let the peace that comes from Christ rule in your hearts.

My Experience

In my case, after twenty years of marriage, almost four years of serious cyclical emotional abuse, and eleven months of daily abuse, my husband began pressuring me to tell the children he'd never abused me. For me, this was the straw that broke the camel's back. I knew it was not true, and I knew I could never, in good conscience, say this to my children. After all, they would know it was not true.

I realized by giving in to my husband's abuse over many years I had allowed evil into my home. I had allowed my husband to treat me abusively and, even worse, I had allowed my children to live with his example

159

of what a "Christian" father looked like. I had also allowed him to be his worst self by not saying no to his abuse. I had not followed Paul's advice in Romans 12:21:

Do not be overcome by evil, but overcome evil with good.

After seeking help from my church twice, and praying daily for almost five years that God would work a miracle in my marriage, I had to make the decision to leave my husband. From the moment I made the decision, I became really frightened. I fully understood I was being seriously abused. I realized his abuse was escalating, and he was in fact now physically abusive. I was also aware that most abusers become even more violent when faced with the reality their wife may leave them. What I needed to do, then, was plan my escape carefully.

CHAPTER 26:

What is the Best Way to Prepare to Leave?

Do Your Research *Before* You Leave or Ask Him to Leave

If you feel you have enough time before making an escape, making some preparations in advance will help you in the long run. If you are afraid for your life, please leave as soon as possible, forgo the planning. Just get to a safe place like your nearest women's crisis center.

When I first separated from my husband, I had very good support from the legal system. The main reason this was true was because I educated myself before I acted. Once I realized my husband was seriously emotionally abusing me, and I was no longer safe in my own home, I began to research the best course of action.

I began my search by calling the National Domestic Violence Hotline (1-800-799-7233). The domestic violence advocate who answered the phone gave me the number of my local women's crisis center. They recommended I come in and see one of their counselors, which I did as soon as I possibly could. After a few visits, I decided I should see a lawyer. The crisis center had a sister organization, which was a free legal service. I asked the operator at the legal service for attorney recommendations. Thankfully, I could afford to hire a private lawyer. She gave me the phone numbers of three attorneys. I then told her I needed the strongest one (I knew I'd be in for a battle against my husband). She then narrowed the list for me, and gave me the name of the best lawyer.

I made an appointment with the lawyer as soon as I could. She offered to meet with me for a flat fee of $100.00. She spent almost two hours with me for that price (less than her usual hourly rate). I told her my story as briefly as possible. She nodded her head when I spoke, and listened intently. As soon as she started speaking, a huge wave of relief poured over me. She didn't talk down to me as if I was crazy. She obviously believed I was being abused.

I asked her for references, which I checked. I also met with another attorney a friend had recommended, to make sure I was making the wisest choice. The second attorney wasted a lot of my time (and money) discussing her own life. She didn't listen carefully to what I was saying, but was more interested in telling me her thoughts. I chose the first attorney, and never regretted my decision.

Legal advice is available for women who cannot afford private attorneys. Many churches will also help with legal costs, or your church may have an attorney who would donate his/her time. If this is the case, please make sure the attorney is knowledgeable about domestic violence. Whatever you do, I recommend getting the best advice you possibly can, even if it seems expensive at the time. You won't regret it.

Acquire Proof Before Leaving

As I said earlier, if you are afraid for your life, do not wait. Call the National Domestic Violence Hotline immediately, 1-800-799-SAFE (7233) or 1-800-787-3224 (TTY). If you feel safe waiting while you are gathering legal information, you should also try to gather proof of the abuse. You

Lifesaver from a Survivor

Don't tell your husband you are gathering proof, and don't feel guilty about it. Your safety depends on this.

might start by keeping a journal, in your own handwriting. I encourage you to hide this carefully so he cannot find it. Perhaps a friend can keep it in her home for you.

I never thought my husband would read my journal, so I kept it in my night table. A few months before I left, I was shocked when he told me he'd read my journals, and they were all "a bunch of crap." Once I decided to leave I started another journal, and kept it very well hidden. Thank the Lord he did not destroy any of my journals!

One of your best tools will be calls you've made to the police. Also, keep track of any of your visits to the doctor or emergency room. If it is possible, take pictures of any bruises or cuts you receive. Also, befriend your neighbors, so they can testify for you about hearing loud arguments or loud noises coming from your home.

You may also consider making an audiotape of him abusing you. I tried this, but the quality was poor, and the most damaging things he said were completely muffled. But be careful: in some states, taping someone without their knowledge is illegal. Each state has its own laws about this. Ask your lawyer about the laws in your state.

If he emails you, texts you, or leaves you voice messages, save them. If you can print the messages, do it, and give them to a friend for safekeeping. He can easily erase old emails if he feels you might use them against him. In the same way, save anything he writes you.

Don't Feel Guilty About Making a Safety Plan for Yourself

After I had decided to leave, but was in the preparation stage, I really struggled with whether I should tell my husband I was planning to leave. I felt disloyal going behind his back, gathering proof, and seeking an attorney's counsel.

I finally decided my safety and the future safety of my children was my highest priority. I knew I would be in even greater danger if I allowed him to have any idea of what I was planning.

The brother of one of my friends likened this period of time to a poker game. He said, "You don't want to show what is in your hand before you lay down the cards."

An Example of What Might Happen Without Good Legal Preparation

I have a friend who was not able to research legal options before she separated from her emotionally abusive husband. She found out he had been having affairs, and asked him to leave. As soon as he left, her children began telling her how their father had sexually abused them. She was rightfully afraid for her children, so she took them and left their home, leaving no information about where they went. The first night she left, she went to a women's crisis center, and I felt relieved the center would help them through the process while providing safety for her and her children.

Unfortunately, she didn't feel comfortable at the crisis center, and stayed only one night. She then went to stay with friends. Her husband found her a few weeks later at the children's counselor's office. He met her with the police and a court order to give him the children immediately, which she was forced to do.

A few days later, they had an emergency hearing in front of the county judge. My friend had to scramble to find a lawyer who would take her case.

The judge's mind was completely against my friend. She told my friend that "kidnapping" her children was wrong, and allowed my friend's abusive husband to have full custody for over a year while they went through the court process. I can only imagine the pain she and her children experienced because of this.

In this case, she could have done some things differently to protect herself and her children. I pray if you decide you need to leave your abusive husband, you will have time to do your research before you jump into a bad situation.

CHAPTER 27:

How Can You Escape Safely?

My Escape

When I decided I must separate from my husband, I began making plans in the middle of the night when everyone was asleep. I was having trouble sleeping through the night anyway, because I was so upset and frightened. Also, I had a real dread of what I was contemplating. I was afraid my church would not support me (they didn't). I was afraid if I left the house, my children, who were teenagers with their own car, would not come with me (they probably would not have).

Since I was alone in a quiet house, I was able to research job openings on the Internet, as well as look for an affordable apartment to rent. During our first meeting, I told my lawyer I was planning to move to an apartment. She said immediately, "Oh no, *he* will have to leave." I told her he would not leave willingly. She said, "We'll make him leave." I asked how. She told me she would help me get a temporary civil restraining order from the court. I had never heard of that!

That is exactly what we did. I was able to get the order, and he was barred from the house. The Lord blessed me immeasurably in this way. However, if my children would have gone with me willingly, I would have been happy to leave the house.

I share my experience with you so you are aware that staying in your own home may be an option for you. However, it is apparently quite rare. You will probably have to leave your home, at least initially. The most important thing is that you get the best legal assistance you can find, and that you and your children are safely out of the violence. Remember, a man who has been emotionally abusive may turn physically violent when he realizes you are trying to leave. You need to protect yourself and your children at all costs.

An Escape Described

In the first chapter of *Battered but Not Broken,* Patricia Riddle Gaddis describes a woman she calls Kimberly who had been physically abused for years.[75] Kimberly had absolutely no money of her own. To prepare to leave, she opened a bank account and had the statements sent to a friend's address so her husband would not find out about it. She then began selling some of the expensive clothes her husband had bought her to a consignment store. She also took a small job in her church nursery, after telling her husband she wanted to save money for Christmas presents.

In addition, Kimberly began sending small boxes of clothing, important papers, and personal keepsakes to an aunt who lived out of state. She feared she would one day have to leave immediately and would be unable to collect all the items that were important to her, which is what happened. Her husband sensed something was different about her, and began asking her over and over about the money she was saving for Christmas presents. He beat her terribly. She was finally able to convince him to go to her locker at church, where she pretended she was hiding the money she was saving. The minute his car disappeared up the road, she got her car keys, her son, and left the state, stopping only to withdraw all her money from her savings account.

What If You Have Children?

One word of caution about leaving the state if you have children: please get legal advice before doing this. I have been told if you are still married and no court orders are in place, nothing restricts a parent taking her children out of her home state. On the other hand, I have heard in many states you might be arrested for kidnapping if you take your children out of state without your husband's consent. Good legal advice will be invaluable to you. If you truly cannot afford any attorney fees, most states have free resources for battered women. Call your local crisis center, or the National Domestic Violence Hotline for information, 1-800-799-SAFE (7233) or 1-800-787-3224 (TTY).

Lifesaver from a Survivor

Taking your children out of your state might be dangerous; you could be arrested for kidnapping. Research the laws in your state.

What If You Have Pets?

Whenever possible, make a safety plan for your pets as well as for your children and yourself. Your abuser may use your pets as a tool to coerce you and your children to come home. If you and your children's lives are in danger, you should leave, but try to consider your pets if at all possible. Some crisis centers may be able to help you find a safe place for your pets. Some states now include pets on restraining orders.

Where Can You Escape?

You may go several places to be safe. Listed below are examples:

Crisis Centers

The positives for going to a women's crisis center are numerous:

- It will be completely safe; your husband will not be able to follow you.

- It will be free; they won't charge you anything.

- You will get around the clock protection, counseling, and assistance.

As with most plans, going to a crisis center has some negatives:

- You will most likely be in a place very different from the home you are leaving, which may be stressful to you and your children. However, if your home was very frightening, different may be a blessing to all of you.

- You will not have friends and family nearby.

- If your son(s) are older than twelve, they may not be allowed in the center.

The crisis center nearest to you may be full. Please call them first. Again, the National Domestic Violence Hotline Number is 1-800-799-SAFE (7233) or 1-800-787-3224 (TTY).

Hotels

If you can afford it, you might prefer to go to a hotel. You will have some privacy, and usually some nice amenities to make your life easier. Please don't go to any hotel you and your husband have been to in the past. It should be a place he will not think to look for you. Also, you can tell the management you will not accept any incoming phone calls or visitors, and why. They protect the privacy of their guests.

Note: your church might be willing to give you the money to stay temporarily in a hotel. You could ask them.

Family

Having the support and protection of your family would be great at this time, but this may not be the best place for you to go for several reasons:

- Your husband will look for you here first. If he finds you, this may put your family in danger.

- Your family may have strong opinions about what you are doing, and may not support your decision to leave. You will have enough concerns without trying to continually explain your decision.

Friends

If you have friends who have been supporting you, and are willing to allow you to stay with them, this may be a good option for you, at least temporarily. However, staying with friends may have some of the same drawbacks that staying with family may have:

- If your husband knows these friends well, he may find you, putting your friends in danger.

- Don't go to your friends if they do not support you completely.

- Being a houseguest for an extended period of time may put a strain on your friendship.

Church Members

Your church may have some members who will offer to allow you to stay with them for a time. This may be a good option, again, if they are completely supportive, and if your husband is unlikely to find you.

Your Own Home

As I said earlier, you may be fortunate enough to stay in your own home. If your husband is willing to leave, or if he is forced to leave because of a restraining order, you may stay in your home, but please take extra precautions:

- Have the police go with you into your home the first time, to make sure he is not hiding.

- Change the locks on every door before going into the house at all.

- Change the code on your garage door openers.

- Keep the doors and windows locked at all times.

- If he has a key to your car, try to get it back from him. If you can't get his key, you can install a steering column device that prevents him from driving the car.

- Keep copies of your restraining order in several places around your home, in case he breaks in and you need to call the police. You will need to show the police your restraining order when they come to the house. You should also keep a copy on your person, and in your car. If the order is modified later, put the updated copy in all these places.

- Have an alarm system installed. If you already have one, change ALL the codes so he cannot disarm it. When you are in the home, turn the alarm ON.

- Other safety measures you can install in your home are devices to record anything said on your home phone, and hidden video cameras by your front door. Get some legal advice before using these, as YOU might get in trouble for taping/filming him without his knowledge.

> *You might escape to:*
>
> - A crisis center
> - A hotel
> - The home of a friend, family, or church member
> - Your own home

Get Help from Your Local Crisis Center

No matter where you choose to go (even if you are able to stay in your own home), you will need all the help you can get. Your local crisis center will most likely have a counseling service, as well as a shelter. They will be able to help you whether you can afford to pay them or not. Their counselors can help you with everything you will need, such as:

- Counseling
- Legal advice
- Finding a job
- Day care
- A place to live
- Food
- Clothing
- Money, etc.

Be Careful of Leaving a Trail Where He Can Find You

Your husband can try to find you in a variety of ways. Make sure you think through all of these things:

- **Home phone or cell phone**—If his name is also on these accounts, he can get a list of everyone you have called, even local phone numbers. Also, cell phones have tracking devices in them, so you can be traced through your cell phone. Leave your cell phone behind, and get a new one through a new cell phone company so he cannot call and get your number.

- **Credit card receipts**—If he is on your credit card, or if your statement comes to your home, he will get a listing of every place you use it, including the hotel where you may be staying.

- **Bank withdrawals**—If he is on your bank account, or if your statements come to your home, he will be able to get a list of every check you write,

Your husband might find you via:

- Phone bills
- Credit card bills
- Bank statements
- Email or social media
- Friends
- Stalking you

or every ATM withdrawal you make, and the location of the withdrawals.

- If you need to call him, or someone he is close to, for any reason, **be careful where you call from.** If you call his cell phone, or a number that has caller ID, the number you are calling from will be displayed for him to see. Be aware that even if he doesn't have caller ID, he can get this information from the phone company. In addition to protecting you and your children, you must also protect the friends, family, or hotel where you are staying. **Note:** If you have received a restraining order from him, you should *not* call him for any reason. By calling him, authorities will believe you are not serious about protection from him.

- **Change your email address** so he cannot contact you that way or, if he is allowed to contact you by email, get another account to communicate with everyone else and block his account from accessing your new account. This way, if he bombards you with emails, you can choose when/if to look at them. He may also have the password to your current email account, and would be able to see what emails you are sending and receiving from others.

- **Consider whether to change your social media accounts.** If you completely stop using them, he might be suspicious and stalk you with even more vigor. Also, if your social media interactions are very important to you, this may feel like one more loss to you. However, he will be able to track your movements via your Facebook and other social media accounts. For example, if you post a status describing your new job, or your favorite new restaurant, he will know where to look for you. If you post a picture of yourself posing in front of a landmark in the new city you have just moved to, he will know where you now live. Even if *you* don't post things like this, your friends might. If your husband is "friends" on social media with your friends, he might find you through them. So consider very carefully whether to use social media at all, and if you do use it, how to do so wisely.

- **Remind friends to never give out new contact information**, and trust very few! A friend of mine had "friends" who told her husband where she was, saying, "Well, he is a Christian."

- **If you are working, he could wait for you and follow you** to your safe house when you leave work. Notify Human Resources of your situation. They may even decide a security guard is warranted for everyone's protection. He may also wait for you at your church, day care, kid's school, your school, gym, or any other places you or your children regularly go. You might want to change as many of these as you can. Also, you could enlist the help of any security guards who work at these places. In addition, it would be wise to leave work at different times each day, and drive to the crisis center or other locations by a different route each day.

Pray for God's protection over you and your children. The following are verses you can cling to.

Psalm 27:1–3

The LORD is my light and my salvation—
whom shall I fear?
The LORD is the stronghold of my life—
of whom shall I be afraid?

When evil men advance against me
to devour my flesh,
when my enemies and my foes attack me,
they will stumble and fall.

Though an army besiege me,
my heart will not fear;

Proverbs 3:5–6

Trust in the LORD with all your heart
and lean not on your own understanding;

in all your ways acknowledge him,
and he will make your paths straight.

Proverbs 2:12–14

Wisdom will save you from the ways of wicked men,
from men whose words are perverse,

who leave the straight paths
to walk in dark ways,

who delight in doing wrong
and rejoice in the perverseness of evil.

Note: if you have been writing your answers to these questions in this book, I caution you to be very careful to keep the book where your husband can't find it, especially when answering the questions in this section.

1. Are you afraid of your husband?

2. Do you think leaving him is in your best interest?

3. If you have decided you should leave him, what are the steps you can take now to prepare yourself? Do you have any proof of the abuse? If not, how can you get some proof?

4. Where would be the safest place for you to escape to?

5. If you have pets, what kind of plan should you make for them?

6. When would be the best time for you to make your escape?

 *A Drink of Water for the Journey*

"Fear and trembling have beset me; horror has overwhelmed me. I said, 'Oh, that I had the wings of a dove! I would fly away and be at rest—

I would hurry to my place of shelter, far from the tempest and storm.'"

(Psalm 55:5–6, 8)

SECTION 8:

Preparing for Legal Issues

CHAPTER 28:

Should You Try to Get a Restraining Order?

What Is a Civil Restraining Order?

For many women, getting a civil restraining order (sometimes also called a protection order) may be very helpful. A judge will issue this order if the abused woman can prove she has reason to be afraid of her partner. The initial order is usually only temporary, and lasts for around two to four weeks. Her partner is not in the courtroom when the initial temporary order is issued.

The temporary order will have language similar to the following, stating the restrained person is not allowed to:

- Harass, stalk, injure, intimidate, threaten, molest, or use any physical force against the protected party.

- Contact the party, nor is he allowed to contact her through any third party except an attorney.

- He must keep a distance of 100 yards (or some specified distance) away from her.

- He may not enter a home, workplace, school, or any other place she might be.

Her children may or may not be added to the order, depending on whether the judge feels they also need protection.

The temporary order will be fairly easy to obtain. A process server or law enforcement officer must serve it to the restrained person. If the restrained person does any of the actions listed on the restraining order, the protected person (you) are allowed to call the police, and if you can prove he has in fact broken the restraining order, he can be arrested. The temporary order can be extended if it can be tied to an ongoing legal action, such as a legal separation, divorce, or child custody proceeding. In other words, you may not have to petition for a permanent order during the time you are working out the details of a legal separation, divorce, or child custody; the temporary order might remain in effect during that time.

A permanent restraining order is much more difficult to get. Before the temporary order expires, both parties must appear before the judge, and each gets to provide their side of the case. In cases of emotional abuse, and even in cases of minor physical abuse, a judge will rarely order a permanent restraining order. A permanent restraining order usually requires a lot of proof of serious physical abuse before a judge will order one. However, if the abuser has broken the temporary order and the police have been called, receiving a permanent order will be easier. In many states, the restrained person can petition the court to have the permanent restraining order removed every four years. The result is entirely up to the judge.

> *If you have received a restraining order, **never** try contacting the restrained person. Doing so appears to the court as if you were not really afraid.*

Note that if you are the protected party, you should never try to contact the restrained person, except in the ways the restraining order allows. For example, you may be allowed to email your husband concerning scheduling the children. Other than this, contact with him would appear to the court that you were not really afraid of him.

Should You Try to Get a Civil Restraining Order?

A civil restraining order could be very helpful to you if your husband is the type of person who would be apt to follow an order like this. Many abusive men go against the order until they have the consequence of being arrested for breaking the restraining order. After that, many will follow the order.

However, some abusers will become much more violent when issued a restraining order. They will not be deterred in any way by the threat of going to jail. In fact, they see it as a challenge, and may behave much worse than if you simply left. For this type of man, getting a restraining order will not help; it will only make things worse. You are the best judge of your husband's potential reaction to this. Your local women's crisis center can help you think through what is best for your circumstances.

Lifesaver from a Survivor

You are the best judge of your husband's potential reaction. Will he abide by the restraining order, or see it as a challenge?

My Experience

When I decided my husband and I should separate, I sought out a lawyer who was an expert in dealing with domestic violence cases. I described this in detail in Chapter 27. She felt I had a very good chance of getting a temporary civil restraining order against my husband so he would be forced to leave our home. I was absolutely terrified to take this step, but agreed this was the best course of action. I knew my husband would not leave our home unless he was forced. I also thought that if I left, my children would not support my decision, and would stay in our very nice home with my husband. Even though they were aware of a lot of the withholding he had been doing, my husband had kept most of his physical abuse secret from them. He woke me in the night, wrestled me to the ground, and blocked me from leaving rooms, etc., when they were asleep or at school.

Once I had decided to get a restraining order, I had to decide when to have him served with it. He was not working outside the home at that time. I did not want him to receive this at our home, in case the children or I might be there. I was very afraid of his reaction, and did not wish to be anywhere near him when he received the order. I finally decided the only option was to have him served at the university where he was taking classes. This meant I had to move quickly, because the end of the semester was fast approaching.

On a Tuesday morning, I met my attorney at the county courthouse at 9:00 a.m. Before I left my home that morning, I packed bags for my children and myself in case my husband became violent and I was afraid to return home. I also had a chance that the judge would refuse my request, and then I would be forced to leave. I packed everything I thought we would need, school books and papers, contact lenses and solutions, glasses, Bibles, clothes, shoes, etc. You name it, I packed it.

When I arrived at the courthouse, my attorney and I sat in a courtroom waiting for our turn. In the room with us were many strangers who had come to plead their case for speeding tickets, failure to pay child support, etc. Since our case was more urgent, they took us right away.

My attorney stated briefly I was seeking a restraining order. The judge asked me why I felt I needed one. Thankfully, my attorney had written up a brief outlining my husband's most abusive behaviors. These included:

- My husband telling me he wanted me to die.
- Pictures of the bruise he left on my hand when he hit me with a belt.
- Waking me in the middle of the night to scream at me (I could list specific dates this had happened).
- Leaving red finger marks on my daughter (I had a picture of this).
- Refusing to tell me the doctor's instructions when one of our sons received a head injury.
- The fact he did not speak to me (except to be abusive) for an entire year.

I stood up in front of twenty people I'd never met and shared all the abuse I'd been trying to hide from the world and myself. It brought to mind Luke 12:2–3:

> *There is nothing concealed that will not be disclosed, or hidden*
>
> *that will not be made known. What you have said in the dark*
>
> *will be heard in the daylight, and what you have whispered in*
>
> *the ear in the inner rooms will be proclaimed from the roofs.*

Even though this was a difficult step for me, and potentially embarrassing, I had complete peace during this time. I know the Lord was carrying me in His arms that day.

My attorney had suggested I ask the judge to grant my husband only therapeutic visitation with the children initially. The judge decided to order my husband have *no* contact with the children for the two weeks the temporary order was in place. So, the children were placed on the restraining order as well, much to our surprise. My husband was ordered to leave the marital home, and to only return to get things he needed with a police escort.

I waited in my car for a few hours until a process server who my attorney had hired could serve my husband with the restraining order. He was served next to his car in the parking lot (I'd given them his license plate number). The process server called my cell phone immediately to say, "Watch out, he's really mad." The second I hung up, my phone rang again. It was my husband.

Reporting Him for Breaking the Restraining Order

I answered my cell phone and said firmly but quietly into it, "You've just broken the restraining order, and I'm calling the police." I hung up and dialed 911. The police came and took a report (about one and a half hours later). They explained that since he didn't actually speak to me, he hadn't technically broken the order.

At least he didn't call me back ever again, as long as the order was in effect. However, he did break the order multiple times in the first few weeks:

- He called my children and spoke to them, asking them to talk me into letting him come home.

- He called my parents and emailed them, though asking a third party to intervene was strictly prohibited by the order.

- He emailed me with many sweet words of love, also strictly prohibited. We were to have email communication only about scheduling for the children. After the initial couple of weeks, he also emailed me trying to shame me, asking if the "Holy Spirit had convicted me yet that I was wrong about him and the children."

He came into the gym where my sons and I were working out and walked within ten feet of me. He'd been ordered to keep a distance of 100 yards away from me.

I could tell by these actions that he was not taking the restraining order seriously. At each infraction, I spoke to my attorney, asking her what I should do. Each time she advised me to make a report to the police, but I was afraid to. Finally I decided I must.

Since I had written proof of many of the infractions (emails), I printed them and went to the police station, where two officers took my report. I was very pleased they took it so seriously, even though the infractions were not physically threatening.

I assumed they would call him and say something like "Sir, you must stop contacting your wife; you have a restraining order against you." Instead, they told me the case would go to an investigator, and a warrant would probably be issued for his arrest.

Waiting for Him to be Arrested

Over the next few weeks, an investigator called me several times asking for clarification. A few weeks later, I was still waiting to hear what the investigator had decided. I was unable to reach him, though I left multiple messages. I finally spoke to his supervising sergeant, and was told a standing warrant was out for my husband's arrest.

Time seemed to go very slowly then. I was afraid they would go to his new apartment, or pull him over on the road, when he was with my children (the restraining order for the children was lifted after a few weeks, so my husband was spending time with them). Two months went by and nothing happened. I finally called the police department again, asking what was going on. I was told that since it was a nonviolent offense, the police would not actively search for him. Instead, if he got a speeding ticket, or was contacted by the police for anything, they would look up his record and arrest him then. I couldn't believe that! That could be years from now, or tomorrow!

My attorney told me not to worry. She explained that when we went to court for temporary orders in the legal separation case in two months, they would arrest him when he walked into the courtroom.

His Arrest at Temporary Orders

Five months after I received the temporary restraining order, and four months after I reported him to the police, we met with a mediator. My attorney told my husband's attorney about the warrant for my husband's arrest for defying the temporary restraining order. This gave him over three weeks to turn himself in and spend the one night he was going to have to spend in jail. Two of those weeks I was with the children. My hope was he would do this quietly, so the children would not need to know their father had been taken to jail. He chose not to do this. Instead, he waited until our court date. The court date was during his parenting week, so the children were sleeping at his house that night.

Just before we went into the courtroom, my attorney spoke to my husband and his attorney. She reiterated that if he appeared in the courtroom, he was going to be arrested. My husband looked at her boldly and basically said, "Bring it on." I'm sure he still did not believe anyone was going to hold him accountable for his actions.

We all went into the courtroom. The judge walked in with a county sheriff. Her first words were, "Apparently everyone but the Court is aware a warrant is out for [my husband's] arrest. Any reason why the sheriff should not take him into custody right now?" Everyone agreed we should try to settle the remaining issues before he was taken away. The Child and Family Investigator (CFI) made her recommendation that we should have joint decision making in all areas affecting the children. The judge pulled open her huge law book with all the state statutes, and began reading from it. "According to the statute, 'In cases of domestic violence, it is deemed inappropriate to have joint decision making.' I am not saying domestic violence was in this case, but a temporary restraining order was issued, and the sheriff is here to arrest him for breaking it." She then turned to the CFI and said, "I cannot order it, but I highly recommend an expert in domestic violence be added to this case so that these issues can be thoroughly investigated." Then she said, "In the meantime, I am ordering full decision making except for extracurricular activities be given to the mother in this case."

The judge then worked out with the CFI to go with me to my husband's apartment to bring the children home, "since he will be spending the night in jail."

I cannot even begin to describe the pain my children experienced during the next week, all because my husband refused to acknowledge he was being held accountable for his actions. I feel sure he wanted the children to know "their mother put their father in jail." He used this line over and over for the next several months.

What is a Criminal Restraining Order?

Committing domestic violence is a crime, which is why my husband was taken to jail for a night. Once a man is arrested, he will be treated as a defendant, and will be put into the court system. He will have to make a plea to the district attorney and appear before a judge. When his case is over, he will probably be put on probation, and may have to serve some type of sentence. This could be a court mandated treatment program for abusers, or possibly jail time.

After he has been arrested for domestic violence, in some states a man will automatically be issued a criminal restraining order, which reads very much like a civil restraining order. This is true whether he is arrested for breaking a civil restraining order or whether he is arrested during the act of committing domestic violence. The criminal restraining order will be in effect whether or not a civil restraining order is in place. Once his case is finished, the criminal restraining order may be dismissed, extended for a certain number of years, or made permanent.

Do the Police Always Follow Restraining Orders?

I was fortunate to live in city where judges and police take domestic violence seriously. I have friends who were not as fortunate. The abuser of one friend convinced police officers in their city that his wife had forged her restraining order. I have heard many stories where courts refused to issue restraining orders, even when the woman's safety was obviously at risk.

I pray the courts and police in your area will do their jobs and protect you. If they don't, you can always appeal to those higher up the chain of command. No matter what you do, I recommend you appeal to the top of the chain of command, and pray to the Lord for protection. Here is a prayer you might pray, written by David when he was being chased through the wilderness by King Saul:

Psalm 57

Have mercy on me, O God, have mercy on me,

for in you my soul takes refuge.

I will take refuge in the shadow of your wings

until the disaster has passed.

I cry out to God Most High,

to God, who fulfills his purpose for me.

He sends from heaven and saves me,

rebuking those who hotly pursue me;

Selah

God sends his love and his faithfulness.

I am in the midst of lions;

I lie among ravenous beasts—

men whose teeth are spears and arrows,

whose tongues are sharp swords.

Be exalted, O God, above the heavens;

let your glory be over all the earth.

They spread a net for my feet—

I was bowed down in distress.

They dug a pit in my path—

but they have fallen into it themselves.

Selah

My heart is steadfast, O God,

my heart is steadfast;

I will sing and make music.

Awake, my soul!

Awake, harp and lyre!

I will awaken the dawn.

I will praise you, O Lord, among the nations;

I will sing of you among the peoples.

For great is your love, reaching to the heavens;

your faithfulness reaches to the skies.

Be exalted, O God, above the heavens;

let your glory be over all the earth.

CHAPTER 29:

What Might a Court Case Be Like?

Working with a Mediator

In my state, spouses who are asking for legal separation or divorce are asked to agree on all financial and parenting decisions shortly after filing for separation. If they cannot agree, they are required to meet with a mediator. We went through this process on two separate occasions. Because a restraining order was in effect, my attorney and I were allowed to be in a separate room from my husband and his attorney.

We spent many hours coming to agreements. My attorney offered to type up all the agreements, but when she presented them to his attorney, my husband backed out on all he had agreed upon. Hence, the mediation process was a complete waste of time and money.

Temporary Orders

In some states, you will have an opportunity to appear before a judge fairly early in the process to decide things such as financial issues and parenting time. This is called temporary orders. It usually is a fairly short hearing, and you likely will not have to wait very long to get this time before a judge. The decision of this judge will only remain in effect until the case is ready to be finished and you have a final hearing, which is called final orders.

Moving from Legal Separation to Divorce

When I first got the restraining order, I filed for legal separation. I wanted to leave the door open for reconciliation if my husband was willing to do the hard work required to make changes in his life. My husband immediately began pressuring me through my pastor (the same one I had gone to for help the year before) to drop the legal separation proceedings. They both insisted a legal separation was no different than a divorce. I disagreed; after all, you cannot remarry until you are actually divorced. To me, that was a BIG difference.

As we moved through the year of the court process, I held my ground. When the time finally arrived for final orders, my husband petitioned for divorce. Our state is a "no fault" state, and divorces cannot be "contested." Suddenly, I found myself about to be divorced.

Final Orders

When the time came for final orders in our case, about a year after the temporary restraining order was issued, most of the decisions had already been finalized. We had already agreed to split our assets equally, and the children (unfortunately) were switching back and forth between our houses for a week at a time, so parenting time had already been decided. However, I petitioned for a permanent restraining order, and sole decision making for the children. I felt I needed the security of a long-term restraining order to remain safe, and I felt my husband was not capable of making appropriate decisions for the children, based upon the type of parent he had been in the past.

In our state, you can hire an independent judge. We decided to do this so we could choose our judge, and also so the hearing would be sooner. Our hearing took three entire days. The first day the three counselors involved spoke—mine, his, and the children's. In addition, our Child and Family Investigator spoke, and several people I called "the dog and pony show" came. The "dog and pony show" was several people from our old church, my sons' coaches, and friends of my husband, who said what a kind person he was, what a great dad, and a wonderful Christian. Of course, not one of them had ever witnessed the way he treated me at home. Unfortunately, my lawyer didn't think character witnesses for me was necessary, which turned out to be a mistake.

The second day, I was grilled for seven hours about why I felt I needed a permanent restraining order. I had almost 1,000 pages of journals covering the last five years of the marriage, as well as about 150 emails he had sent me during the last year. I had compelling evidence he had emotionally abused me, and was becoming physically abusive as well.

On the final day, my husband had his turn to talk. His attorney objected to every line of questioning my attorney began. Almost without fail, the judge agreed with the objection, and my attorney had to stop. Even with that, my attorney caught my husband lying at least once, and he had to admit he was lying. Several other times, I knew he was lying, but it was my word against his.

Because the evidence was so compellingly in my favor, I was shocked when the judge (a woman) denied my request for a permanent restraining order, and ordered we have joint decision making in all areas dealing with the children. I simply could not believe my ears. I walked out of the room at a quick pace, and proceeded to sob my heart out in the bathroom. Both the judge and the CFI (also a woman, who had stated this outcome was "best for the children") asked my attorney if I was "all right," a total of six times between them. My attorney answered over and over again, "No."

Praise God I still had a criminal restraining order in effect, since he had broken the civil restraining order and was sent to jail overnight. I was unclear how long that would last, however.

I was so angry and hurt. I have tried to figure out why I was upset to the point that I did not get to sleep that night until 4:00 a.m. I was upset, obviously, that I no longer had the restraining order. But what upset me most was how the judge and the CFI sat for hours listening to me describe in detail all the frightening things he'd done, and basically said to me, "We don't believe you," or worse, "We don't care." I also was taken completely by surprise, since the other two judges I'd been in front of had sided so completely with me.

Were Any Blessings in All of This?

The blessing in all this was I was literally thrown back into the arms of the Lord, who was my only hope and Savior. What a safe place to be. A friend, who had walked with me through all the years of abuse, sent me an email with Psalm 91 paraphrased to be speaking directly to me. I enclose it as a comfort to you as well.

"I don't know why this has happened to you (she said), but, we do know these things:

You dwell in the shelter of the Most High,

you can find rest (only) in the shadow of the Almighty.

He is your (only) refuge and your fortress,

your God in whom I know you trust!

Surely He will save you from the fowler's snare

and from the deadly pestilence.

He will cover you with His feathers,

and under His wings (alone) you will find refuge;

His faithfulness will be your shield and rampart.

You will not fear the terror of night,

nor the arrow that flies by day,

nor the pestilence that stalks in the darkness,

nor the plague that destroys at midday.

If you make the Most High your dwelling—

even the Lord, who (I know) is your refuge—

Then no harm will befall you,

no disaster will come near your tent (including your children).

For He will command His angels concerning you
(and your children)

to guard you in all your ways;

they will lift you up in their hands,

so that you will not strike your foot against a stone.

'Because Caroline loves me,' says the Lord, 'I will rescue her;

I will protect her, for she acknowledges my name.

She will call upon me, and I will answer her;

I will be with her in trouble,

I will deliver her and honor her.

With long life will I satisfy her

and show her my salvation!'

Climb up into His arms and try to sleep there! I am praying for you. I love you,

Your sister in Christ."

The Outcome of the Criminal Case

At the time of our divorce, the criminal case had been pending for close to a year. My ex-husband had been before a district attorney three times and had convinced her to put off settling his case. After the final orders were given in the civil court, he finally settled with the district attorney. I had sent the district attorney a victim impact statement at the beginning of my ex-husband's criminal case. This statement briefly outlined the abusive behavior he had committed before the restraining order, and how I was affected by his breaking the order. In the victim impact statement, I asked the Court to assign him to a nine-month treatment program for abusers offered in our city.

The day my ex-husband and his criminal attorney met at the court, the district attorney called me to get my thoughts on the agreement she was offering. I told her I was requesting he be sentenced to nine months of treatment for abusers. She told me the previous junior district attorney had said he could do a twenty-week anger management course. She did not think she could convince him to agree to a nine-month course. As a result my husband received a suspended sentence, was told to take the twenty-week course, and I was given a very weak restraining order. It stated, "You shall not harass, injure, molest, intimidate, threaten, retaliate against, or tamper with any witness to or victim of the acts you are charged with committing. You shall not possess or control a firearm or other weapon, and you will comply with any civil restraining orders." Of course, no civil restraining orders were in effect any longer. Basically, he was to treat me as he would anyone on the planet.

Needless to say, I was quite distressed about this turn of events. Thankfully, I had already been on my knees begging for protection from the Lord, and asking Him to help me forgive all those who I felt had let me down in the court process. Praise Him; He helped me through this as well, by giving me the following Psalm:

Psalm 37:1–11

Do not fret because of evil men
or be envious of those who do wrong;

for like the grass they will soon wither,
like green plants they will soon die away.

Trust in the LORD and do good;
dwell in the land and enjoy safe pasture.

Delight yourself in the LORD
and he will give you the desires of your heart.
Commit your way to the LORD; trust in him and he will do this:

He will make your righteousness shine like the dawn,
the justice of your cause like the noonday sun.

Be still before the LORD and wait patiently for him;
do not fret when men succeed in their ways,
when they carry out their wicked schemes.

Refrain from anger and turn from wrath;
do not fret—it leads only to evil.

For evil men will be cut off,
but those who hope in the LORD will inherit the land.

A little while, and the wicked will be no more;
though you look for them, they will not be found.

But the meek will inherit the land
and enjoy great peace.

No matter the outcome of your court case, God is still sovereign. You may not be vindicated in this lifetime, but God will one day demonstrate He knows the truth of what has happened to you.

CHAPTER 30:

Will You Get Full Custody of Your Children?

In some states today, custody is called "parenting time." In other words, how much parenting time (per week or per month) does each parent get with the children? An abusive man should not get parenting time with his children. However, this was not my experience. By all accounts, abusive men often get a lot of parenting time with their children. I will describe my experience as an example.

What Does Working with a Child and Family Investigator Look Like?

Ten days after I received the temporary restraining order, my husband and his attorney met my attorney and me in my attorney's office (in separate rooms). I was able to keep the temporary restraining order because I had filed for legal separation. Otherwise, I would have had to petition for a permanent restraining order right then, which is more difficult to get.

During that meeting, we agreed to get a Child and Family Investigator for our case. This person is charged with determining the best interest of the children. My attorney agreed to use a CFI who supposedly had training in domestic violence. I lived to regret the choice we made.

I met with the CFI, who was a very sweet Christian woman. I was lulled into believing she was my friend. This was a bad mistake on my part. I told her things about my insecurities as a mother, and I had not been a perfect wife. These words came back to haunt me when she made her recommendations to the Court at final orders. Another thing I wish I had done differently was put on more of a show when she came for a home visit. My kids just went about their business while I spoke to her. I heard later my husband had engaged in a "rousing game of Boggle" when she visited his apartment. This led her to conclude he was a more "hands on" parent than I was. One of my friends was given good advice. She was told to treat the visitation like a house showing, and pull out all the stops! Impress the heck out of the CFI. Also, any time you talk to ANYONE related to a court case, less is more. Keep things close to the vest. Better to have them ask more questions than for you to give too much.

How Does the Court Decide If the Children Needed Therapeutic Visitation?

My husband and I both met with and chose a Christian counselor for the children. Initially, his role was to meet with my husband and children for their therapeutic visitation. Sorry to say he was inexperienced with domestic violence. Much to my surprise, my children told him repeatedly they loved their dad, missed him, and he was not abusive to them. This was the first of many shocks I received during the next year. In about two weeks, the counselor recommended our children didn't need therapeutic visitation, and they could see their father alone anytime.

How Did the CFI Come to Her Decision?

Our CFI spent about a month investigating our case. Even though I gave her the phone numbers of many neighbors who had witnessed my husband berating our sons in the front yard because they didn't throw a ball correctly, she never called a single one of them. She said she had "prayed about it," and decided living one week with me, and the entire next week with my husband was the best thing. I was absolutely stunned by her decision. Thank the Lord my attorney told me her decision a few hours before I met with her to hear the decision.

Tips from an Expert

When searching for an expert, such as a counselor, attorney, CFI, etc. to help you through your journey, credentials and experience in domestic violence and child welfare are much more important than whether the professional is a Christian or not.

I could barely breathe; I was so shocked and upset. I could not believe a Christian woman would give equal parenting time to my abuser. I was horrified at the thought of my children being alone with him for a week at a time. My attorney counseled me that I could not really fight this, since any judge would take the recommendation of the CFI. I was, consequently, forced to allow this to happen. The next week, my children began moving each weekend from house to house.

Child Custody Practices in the United States and Canada

Lundy Bancroft works to increase the rights of abused mothers and their children in the US court system. The following is taken from his website:[76]

"Our society is currently giving mothers a powerful and crazy-making mixed message. First, it says to mothers, 'If your children's father is violent or abusive to you or to your children, you should leave him in order to keep your children from being exposed to his behavior.' But then, if the mother does leave, the society many times appears to do an abrupt about-face, and say, 'Now that you are spilt up from your abusive partner, you must expose your children to him. Only now you must send them alone with him, without you even being around anymore to keep an eye on whether they are okay.'

"What do we want? Do we want mothers to protect their children from abusers, or don't we?

"The sad result of this double-bind is many mothers, who take entirely appropriate steps to protect their children from exposure to abuse, are being insulted by court personnel, harshly and unethically criticized, and ridiculed in custody evaluations and psychological assessments, and required to send their children into unsupervised contact or even custody with their abusive fathers. And sometimes, these rulings are coming in the face of overwhelming evidence the children have both witnessed abuse and suffered it directly, evidence that would convince any reasonable and unbiased person the children were in urgent need of protection. Family courts across the US and Canada appear to be guilty day in and day out of reckless endangerment of children.

"I wish the 'justice system' dispensed justice, but where it comes to child custody litigation involving abusive fathers, outcomes are mixed at best. With adequate knowledge and planning, and especially if you are among the fortunate mothers who are able to obtain competent legal representation from a lawyer who understands what abusers are like as parents, you may be able to keep your children on the path to healing. If your case goes poorly, you can still find ways to help your children feel your love and support surrounding them, and give them the strength to survive their father's destructiveness. But regardless of the outcome you experience personally, you might want to keep the following points in mind:

"The custody system in the US and Canada is broken. You are not the only person who has experienced unhealthy and biased responses, and you are not the crazy, paranoid, vindictive person they may be painting you as.

"Other women need your help to change the system, so that protective mothers start receiving proper respect for their rights and their children's rights.

"Many women have found when they become active in the protective parents movement, raising their voices loudly for the custody rights of mothers who have been battered or whose children have been sexually abused, their own healing leaps forward."

I know Lundy Bancroft's words paint a dismal picture. My own experience in the court system, and that of many women I know, is not encouraging. Lundy recommends women bond together to help each other, saying this can bring healing. I would also encourage you in the following way: If you are in an abusive relationship right now and you have children, your children are living with the abuse every day. They never escape it. Furthermore, when you stay in the abuse, you are telling your children that abuse is OK, and normal. However, when you leave the abuse, you give them the message that abuse is *not* OK, and *not* normal. You give your children a chance to see a life (yours) without abuse.

The time they spend with you will be a great contrast to the time they spend with their manipulative, abusive father. Even if at first they don't understand what caused you to leave him, they will eventually understand this as time goes by. The time they spend with you, especially if you invest time and energy becoming emotionally healthy, will help them grow into healthy adults themselves. It will break the chain of domestic violence in the next generation.

Lifesaver from a Survivor

Though your children may be forced to spend time alone with your abuser, the time they spend with you will help them grow into healthy adults themselves— breaking the chain of domestic violence in the next generation.

1. Do you think you would have enough evidence to persuade a judge to grant you a temporary restraining order?

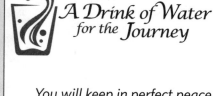

A Drink of Water for the Journey

You will keep in perfect peace

him whose mind is steadfast,

because he trusts in you.

Trust in the LORD forever,

for the LORD,

the LORD,

is the Rock eternal.

Isaiah 26:3, 4

2. Is your husband the type of man who would become violent after receiving a restraining order, or would he follow it for the most part?

3. Do you think requesting a restraining order would be helpful?

4. How do you think you would handle a court case that went in favor of your abuser? Would you be able to trust the Lord in that circumstance?

5. Do you believe your children would be better off spending time with you away from their abusive father, especially if you made an effort to be emotionally healthy?

SECTION 9:

Finding Joy on the Other Side of Abuse

CHAPTER 31:

How Might You Feel After You Take Your Life Back?

I have told the story of my past to many people. They always listen sympathetically. One day, when I told my story to a new friend, I got a new perspective.

I told her about the morning my husband woke me by ripping the covers off my bed and screaming at me. I told him my heart was pounding, and he said "Good, maybe you'll have a heart attack and die." At that point, I ran out of my house in my nightgown. Later that morning, I went to Wal-Mart and bought a change of clothes for myself and all my children and a Rubbermaid bucket to store them in. From that moment forward, that Rubbermaid bucket was always in the back of my car, ready to go. I also slept with my purse and car keys by my bed, and had my portable phone book with me at all times—in other words, I began making my safety plan.

I had always felt this was such a sad moment in my life—that I had to take a step like this to protect myself from my own husband. My new friend helped me see this much differently. She said:

"So, that was the moment you started taking back your life?"

I was so struck by that phrase, "taking back your life." What a great way to describe it and reframe it in my mind! She pointed out that up to that point, I had looked to other people to rescue me: the pastors at my church, the counselor . . . even my husband. I had wanted *them* to make changes in my life so I could be safe. However, at the point I bought clothes for my children and me, I was beginning to take the steps *myself* for my own safety.

I took several more months after going to Wal-Mart, but eventually I took the following steps:

1. Called the National Domestic Violence Hotline.
2. Visited my local women's crisis center for counseling.
3. Called the local crisis center's legal help line for recommendation of a lawyer.
4. Visited the lawyer, and made a plan to get a restraining order.
5. Went with my lawyer to the courthouse, stood before the judge, told him all the abusive things my husband had been doing, and was granted the restraining order.
6. Called the police and reported my husband when he called me the minute he received the restraining order for my children and myself.
7. Went to my children's schools to show their administrators the restraining order and to pick up the children after school.
8. Had the locks changed on my house, and the code changed on my garage doors and alarm system.
9. Called the police and asked them to meet my children and me when we returned home to make sure my husband was not waiting for us in the house.

When we returned home from school that day, my children were understandably upset. One of my daughters had planned to drive her car from school to youth group that evening, and was very angry I made her leave her car in the parking lot and drive immediately home with me. Since the children had also been put on the restraining order and my husband was not allowed to see them, I felt leaving her car was a safer option. Waiting for a locksmith to change the locks on every door and for the police to go through the entire house before we could enter it was very unsettling.

However, once we entered the house I felt an immediate sense of peace. I cooked dinner for the children and myself, and we all sat down together and watched a favorite television show for the first time in quite a while. My husband had kept control of the TV remote, so I had not watched TV in a year. As I sat on the couch with my children around me, I marveled at how wonderful I felt. I could actually *breathe*. That night when I went to bed, I lay in my bed completely alone, and I felt totally at peace. For the first time in years, I was not afraid. I was so thankful.

Proverbs 17:1

Better a dry crust with peace and quiet
than a house full of feasting, with strife.

Proverbs 22:10

Drive out the mocker, and out goes strife;
quarrels and insults are ended.

CHAPTER 32:

How Can You Tell if You Should Reconcile or Not?

If you have gone so far as to step through the Matthew 18 process I described in Chapters 18 through 21, and have separated from your abusive husband, please think long and hard before considering going back to him. A man who is abusive to his wife and/or children will not be healed overnight, or even in one year, or possibly ever. Statistics show very few men who abuse their wives will ever make substantial changes in their behavior. If you do return to him, you may be putting your life or the lives of your children in jeopardy.

Let's consider this further.

Why Do Women Return to Their Abusers?

Here are some common reasons a woman might return to her abusive husband:

1. **Financial concerns for herself and her children**—Documentation states many single mothers live in poverty. If the abused woman is without adequate job skills, she will struggle financially.

2. **Low self-esteem**—A man is able to abuse a woman by gaining power over her. He does this by undermining her self-confidence over a long period of time. The longer she is in the relationship, the lower her self-esteem will be.

3. **Fear of retaliation**—Many women return to their abusive relationships because of fear. They are afraid for their children, their families, and their physical safety.

4. **Battered women often love their husbands, feel sorry for them, and want to help them.**

These four issues are very real for a woman just coming out of an abusive relationship. This is a time to lean on others. Ecclesiastes 4:12 says:

Though one may be overpowered,

two can defend themselves.

A cord of three strands is not quickly broken.

Your local women's crisis center can help you stay strong when your self-esteem is low, and you feel lonely and scared. They can also help you with safety planning and finding a new place to live, as well as finding a (new) job and getting financial help for you and your children. In addition, your family and your church may be able to help you now. This is not a time to be proud—seek the help of others.

Christian women may have more challenges than other women when they leave their abusive marriages:

1. **Lack of support from the Christian community**—Many pastors, and even friends and family of abused women, will not support her decision to leave her husband. This is especially true if little physical abuse has occurred. My pastor did not support my decision. He also told me my husband's abusive behavior was not biblical grounds for divorce.

2. **Many Christians look down on a divorced woman.** I also used to look down on divorced Christians. Feeling like you are a lesser Christian because you are divorced is very painful for a woman who truly loves the Lord and did everything in her power to make her marriage work.

What can you do in these two situations? You can look for other women in your same circumstances, and most likely, you will find some. Ask your church or your local women's crisis center to introduce you to other Christian women who have recently left abusive husbands, or to recommend support groups for Christian women. You can also read books like this one and other books written about abuse for Christian women. See the Appendix.

Beware of Empty Promises

After you leave your abusive husband, he will probably try to get you to come back. He will most likely go into the honeymoon phase of the abuse cycle. I was shocked that even my husband did this. This was the man who did not speak a civil or kind word to me for the entire previous year and had never done the "hearts and flowers" routine before. I received a letter from him in which he said everything I ever wanted to hear him say. He told me he loved me, he was sorry, and he'd never behave like that again.

Even though I was very strong, and truly did not believe him, his letter made me doubt my decision. I had to remind myself of his disrespectful and frightening behaviors over a long period of time that led me to separate from him. I also had a counselor who was an expert in domestic violence and was very familiar with this pattern in abusive men. She correctly predicted this phase would only last a very short time, and soon he would return to trying to control me, which he did. A word of caution: When your abuser suddenly turns nice, he may be stabbing you in the back while your guard is down. The husband of a friend of mine took all their money while he behaved pleasantly toward her, but he left her penniless.

Lifesaver from a Survivor

Once you leave him, your husband may try getting you to come back by going into a "honeymoon" stage. This is not an indication he has changed.

What if He Says He Has Accepted Christ— Should I Return to Him Then?

An abusive husband will likely try anything to get his wife to return to him, even claim to be converted to Christianity. In 2 Timothy, Paul warns us about these people:

> But you must realize that in the last days the times will be full
> of danger. Men will become utterly self-centered, greedy for
> money, full of big words. They will be proud and contemptuous,
> without any regard for what their parents taught them. They
> will be utterly lacking in gratitude, purity and normal human
> affections. They will be men of unscrupulous speech and
> have no control of themselves. They will be passionate and
> unprincipled, treacherous, self-willed and conceited, loving all
> the time what gives them pleasure instead of loving God. **They**

will maintain a facade of "religion", but their conduct will deny

its validity. You must keep clear of people like this.

(2 Timothy 3:1–5,

J.B. Phillips New Testament, emphasis mine)

If your husband *has* recently come to accept Jesus as his Savior and Lord, this will be a big help to him as he makes the difficult changes he will need to make in his life.

What if I Think He Has Completely Changed?

What if you believe your husband really has changed? You can refer back to Chapter 17 where I described how to discern whether an abusive man has really changed or is just in another honeymoon stage of the abuse cycle. In that Chapter, I listed steps he should be willing to take in order to change. This will be even more important if you have gone through all the steps described in the last few chapters, and have actually left your husband. The most important thing he should do before you consider going back to him would be to *complete* a group treatment program for abusers. A man who is unwilling to *complete* his treatment program will fall back into his old patterns and abuse you again.

If your husband is truly willing to make changes, admits he has been abusing you, and is willing to go through extensive group counseling with experts in domestic violence, he may be helped. However, be aware that even if he has the best intentions, he may be unable to change the attitudes and habits that caused him to abuse you. Ask the Lord for discernment and patience with this process. James 1:5 says:

If any of you lacks wisdom,

he should ask God,

who gives generously to all

without finding fault, and it will be given to him.

Reconciliation

What are the chances for true reconciliation? Given the circumstances that led you to separate from your husband, chances are slim he will truly change enough to eliminate abuse in your home in the future. However, in some cases, the two of you together can accomplish reconciliation through the Lord, Luke 1:37 says:

For nothing is impossible with God.

In her book *Keeping the Faith* Marie Fortune writes,

"This is not to say that reconciliation between you and your husband is not possible. Reconciliation is possible if he is willing to get help and stop his violent behavior. In this case, once you see real evidence over a long period of time of real change in him, of true repentance, then you may choose to consider reconciliation. Or you may not. You may feel the damage is too deep between you. In this case, you need not feel guilty for

ifesaver from a Survivor

If you return to your abuser, courts may be less likely to support you if, in the future, he becomes violent again.

getting a divorce. But if you and he do seek to come back together, you will need to consider this a new covenant between you in which you are both really clear that no violence, under any circumstance, will be tolerated. In this case, with God's help, your broken relationship may be healed."[77]

Before returning to your husband, please make sure you are completely at peace with the Lord in the decision. As Philippians 4:7 says:

And the peace of God, which transcends all understanding, will

guard your hearts and your minds in Christ Jesus.

You know your husband better than anyone. Is he apt to promise things he doesn't mean? Is he very good at convincing others outside your family he means well, and has changed? Do *you* believe he has truly *completely* changed? Also, please make sure you have the counsel of many who understand the dynamics of domestic violence. The best person to judge if he has completely changed will be the group leader of his abuse treatment program. If he and others are still afraid for your safety, please wait for a longer period of time before taking this step. Keep in mind, if you return to your abuser the courts might be less likely to support you in the future. Even though many women return to their abusers more than once, then leave again; judges may view your future claims of abuse as suspect.

CHAPTER 33:

Can You Remarry?

This is a difficult question to answer, and many have struggled with what the Bible says about this. Some will say if you are divorced you should never remarry. Others say that in the Old Testament, divorce always came with the right to remarry, thus a husband was required to give his wife a certificate of divorce.

What do theologians say?

In his booklet, *God's Protection of Women: When Abuse is Worse Than Divorce,* Herb Vander Lugt says many Christians believe any person re-married after a divorce lives in a state of perpetual adultery. He believes such persons need to look again at what Moses said on behalf of God in Deuteronomy 24:1–4:[78]

> *If a man marries a woman who becomes displeasing to him*
>
> *because he finds something indecent about her, and he writes*
>
> *her a certificate of divorce, gives it to her and sends her from his*
>
> *house, and if after she leaves his house she becomes the wife of*
>
> *another man, and her second husband dislikes her and writes*
>
> *her a certificate of divorce, gives it to her and sends her from his*
>
> *house, or if he dies, then her first husband,*
>
> *who divorced her, is not allowed to marry her again*
>
> *after she has been defiled. That would be detestable in the eyes*
>
> *of the Lord. Do not bring sin upon the land*
>
> *the Lord your God is giving you as an inheritance.*

In *God's Protection of Women* Vander Lugt writes, "In this passage, a divorce so completely dissolves a marriage that the only restriction imposed on a man who divorces his wife is that he is forbidden from ever marrying her again if she has been remarried, divorced, or even widowed in the meantime."[79]

Concerning this passage, in *Marriage, Divorce, and Remarriage in the Bible*, Jay Adams says the divorce described in this passage would be considered a divorce for "sinful" reasons, and, therefore, not on biblical grounds ("she becomes displeasing to him"). Yet, this wife then becomes the "wife of another man" who is called her "husband." If she was still her first husband's wife "in God's sight," then she would be committing adultery here, and also bigamy. But she is not accused of that. No, she is clearly called the second husband's "wife." Indeed, the first husband is forbidden to marry her "again." This obviously means she is not his wife after their divorce, or during her second marriage.[80]

Because of this passage, and others in the Bible, Jay Adams concludes:

"Even when a separation by divorce occurs as a result of disobedience, divorce broke the marriage. The grounds may be illegitimate, the divorce itself isn't. Believers who wrongly separate by divorce are said to be 'unmarried.' This point appears in all the Scriptures. Speaking of divorced parties as 'still married in God's sight' is quite wrong. The terminology 'still married in God's sight,' is extra-biblical, unbiblical, and harmful."[81]

> Jay Adams says, "Speaking of divorced people as 'still married in God's sight' is quite wrong ... unbiblical and harmful."

What does Mr. Adams mean by the term *extra-biblical*? This means teaching, concepts, or practices that claim to be supported by the Bible, but are based on incorrect interpretation.

Mr. Adams goes on to explain further:

"The view that someone might still be married though divorced leads to many wrong ideas and acts on the part of the divorced parties. For instance, if one thinks two persons are married in God's sight (though divorced), he must, therefore, conclude these parties still have marriage obligations including sexual obligations (1 Corinthians 7:3–5). Believing this, a Christian counselor would find himself in the position of urging his sinfully divorced counselees to continue to live together and to maintain regular sexual intercourse *after divorce* . . . Throwing around such phrases as 'still married in God's eyes' is easy, but it is quite a serious matter to face up to their implications. Indeed, the concept is repugnant."[82]

However, Adams does have some helpful thoughts on how the church is to view remarriage of divorced persons. He points out remarriage is not only allowed, but in some cases encouraged and commanded. It is looked upon favorably in the New Testament (see 1 Corinthians 7:8, 9). He also references Paul's words in 1 Corinthians 7, verses 26 through 28:

Because of the present crisis, I think that it is good for you to

remain as you are. Are you married? Do not seek a divorce. Are

you unmarried? Do not look for a wife. But if you do marry, **you**

have not sinned; *and if a virgin marries, she has not sinned.*

But those who marry will face many troubles in this life,

and I want to spare you this.

(emphasis mine)

He notes that even in times of severe persecution when marriage in general is discouraged, remarrying is not sinful. He says the Scriptures do not support the view that a divorced person is not allowed to remarry. "To call 'sin' what God expressly says is not sin (1 Corinthians 7:28) is a serious error that cannot be ignored. In effect, it amounts to placing the traditions of men above the Word of the Lord by adding restrictions and burdens God has not required us to bear."[83]

> *Jay Adams says, "To call 'sin' what God expressly says is not sin is a serious error . . . it amounts to placing the traditions of men above the Word of the Lord by adding restrictions and burdens God has not required us to bear."*

My Experience

When I first separated from my husband, I was so thrilled to be out from under the abuse that I thought I'd never even consider remarrying.

Within a few months, however, a problem surfaced. I realized I was strongly missing the physical intimacy of marriage. As a Christian woman, I did not consider having a sexual relationship outside of marriage, as many women do. At this point my thoughts were, "Can I never again have sex for the rest of my life?"

Around the same time, I met with a close friend of mine who recommended that if I ever did remarry, I should at least wait until my youngest child left for college (over five years away). Given how I was feeling at that point, I had a hard time envisioning myself being celibate for over five years.

An example of why waiting is a good idea

Shortly after this, I had the chance to speak to my friend Martha, who had remarried when she and her new husband both had young children at home. She told me the only way she could describe the first years of her second marriage was that they were "hell on earth." Her new husband had been divorced less than a year, and was still in court with his ex-wife over custody of their children. At a time when Martha and her new husband should have been bonding and growing their relationship, they had to deal with her children, his children, her ex-husband, and his ex-wife (who liked to call every night at dinner time). Then, as if that weren't enough, they had a baby of their own! She told me that, though their marriage today is very strong, if she had it to do over she'd definitely wait until all the children were out of the house. Waiting began to seem like a good idea to me after all.

Lifesaver from a Survivor

Blending families is hard. Those who get counseling before remarrying have a better chance of withstanding the trials of blending families.

Even though they struggled, God was able to use Martha's situation for His good. She and her husband now have a ministry counseling couples seeking to blend two families together. She says couples who come to them for counseling *before* they marry have withstood the trials of blending their families. Those couples who waited until they were already married and in the midst of conflict with ex-spouses, stepchildren, and each other almost always ended up divorced again.

I share Martha's story to help you think through the difficulties of remarrying. I pray you will be discerning about whether this is what the Lord would have for you, and what His will for the timing of a remarriage might be.

What are some other potential problems with trying to remarry too soon?

One difficulty you may have when you begin looking for a new partner is that you might choose someone who is very much like your ex-husband. Or, you may simply worry you will choose a person just like him. The best way to prevent this is to spend as much time as you need seeking healing for yourself, though this is not an easy process. You must get to the root of why you chose an abusive husband, which may have to do with your family and childhood. Reading books on boundaries and domestic violence can help. Look for my upcoming book, *A Journey to Healing after Emotional Abuse.*

You should also continue surrounding yourself with a support system, including counselors, support groups for abused women, and healthy friendships with other women. Then, if and when the time comes for you to begin courting a new man, these friends and counselors can help you discern whether he is a healthy person, and whether or not he might have a controlling personality. With the knowledge you have gained from your experience, you will understand the wisdom of listening to your friends and family who know you best, and seeking the wisdom of others when choosing a new mate.

CHAPTER 34:

My Prayer for You

As I conclude writing this book, I pray it has been helpful to you. Living with an abusive person is one of the most difficult things a woman might ever experience. The fact that your abuser is someone you love is even more painful. The possibility that other Christians might make this process even harder for you because of their ignorance about domestic violence makes it that much more painful.

My greatest prayer is you will not walk through this process alone. God is here for you, praise Him! His word will guide you and direct you through every difficult step. In addition, the Lord will place around you many people to help you. He will help you find friends, mentors, counselors, and support groups if you will do your part to search for them. Allow the Lord to heal you through the love of others.

Though the courts denied my petition to have sole decision making for the children, and took away my restraining order, God has used even these difficult things to bless my children and me. Though dealing with my ex-husband is difficult, we have been able to come to some decisions that have helped the children. Also, my ex-husband has not tried to physically hurt me—the Lord has kept me safe.

During each step I took, the Lord held my hand. He has given me the right Bible verse on days when I felt I couldn't go on. When I am lonely, a friend will call me or email me. When I'm distressed about dealing with my ex-husband (who is still controlling), my counselor and support group stand by me and help.

The Lord has cared for me financially, given me new friends at my new church, and repaired my relationships at my old church. He has walked with me through writing each page of this book, and has given me a heart for orphans and abused women. He is my father and my husband.

I leave you with my own personal Psalm. I pray it will bless you.

"Caroline's Psalm"

LORD, you are an awesome God.

You are the father of the orphan,

the husband of the widow.

You take an unloved wife,

and give her courage to say "no."

You put friends and angels around her;

You turn the hearts of pagans for her protection.

You give her joy in everyday life;

You give her more friends and children to love.

You give her a home filled with peace,

and a heart filled with joy.

LORD, I praise you and thank you for your

goodness, faithfulness, and strength.

I praise you that you know me, love me,

and will never leave me nor forsake me.

Because of all this, my heart sings,

PRAISE THE LORD!

A Drink of Water
for the Journey

1. What feelings do you think you would have after separating from your abusive husband? Sadness, fear, loneliness, relief, joy?

2. Can you imagine any circumstances in which you would consider reconciling with your abusive husband? If so, what safeguards would you want put in place for yourself first?

3. After reading the Bible verses presented in Chapter 33, do you believe remarrying would be a sin if you divorced your abusive husband? Why or why not?

4. Could you write a Psalm to the Lord in your own words?

And we know that in all things God works for the good of those who love him, who have been called according to his purpose. What, then, shall we say in response to this? If God is for us, who can be against us? Who shall separate us from the love of Christ? Shall trouble or hardship or persecution or famine or nakedness or danger or sword? No, in all these things we are more than conquerors through him who loved us. For I am convinced that neither death nor life, neither angels nor demons, neither the present nor the future, nor any powers, neither height nor depth, nor anything else in all creation, will be able to separate us from the love of God that is in Christ Jesus our Lord.
(Romans 8:28, 31, 35, 37–39)

CHAPTER 34: My Prayer for You

EPILOGUE

Several years have passed since I began writing this book, and a lot has happened to me since then. God has continued to bless me immeasurably more than I could have hoped or imagined (Ephesians 3:20).

Against all hope, my children have managed to survive going back and forth between my house and my ex-husband's. Some of them are still people pleasers, and continue to try to appease their father to keep him from lashing out at them with his temper. Others have seen him for who he is and are able to set more adult boundaries with him. All of them have done very well in school, have good friendships, and have moved closer to the Lord, for which I praise Him.

I have met and married a wonderful man. We met at my new church and, through the help of the Lord, and my friend Martha and her husband, we stepped through our courtship with purity and with our eyes open. They helped us think through all of the potential issues associated with blending a large family (he has several children as well). Because of the preparation we did before we married, the number of issues we had afterward have been minimal compared to those Martha experienced. That is not to say that blending a family is easy—it is *not*.

Praise the Lord; He did not allow us to meet until we both had done the hard work of healing from our first marriages. Then, we entered the relationship slowly, listening to good counsel from godly friends and advisors. Once we discerned we were potentially right for each other, we met with Martha and her husband weekly for several months, going over the materials they developed for couples preparing to blend a family. During that time, we had several friends holding us accountable to keep our relationship pure. This was quite a challenge, especially for me. This was not the way I had conducted myself before I was married the first time. However, I can now say waiting for physical intimacy until after marriage makes a great difference in the amount of passion between the couple once they are married.

Because we conducted our courtship God's way, leaning on His strength, we have been able to overcome *together* any problems arising in our family. The patterns of turning to Him for strength together before we were married have carried over into our marriage in a wonderful way. We have come to truly appreciate God's wisdom in planning the courtship of a couple in the way He did, as well as the wisdom in running a marriage by His design.

When I was in the midst of my abusive first marriage, I would never have dreamed I would be so happy today. At that time in my life, my future looked so dismal and frightening, I wouldn't have been able to conceive of a marriage as joy-filled as the one I now have. I am so thankful to all the friends, and even strangers, who walked with me through my valley of the shadow. Mostly, I praise my Lord and Savior who never left me nor forsook me during my dark moments. Instead, He held my hand each step of the way.

I thank you for reading this book. I know you have suffered many dark days, and may have many more in your future. I pray you grasp our Lord's hand and trust Him to walk alongside you during *your* journey. I am confident He will never leave you, nor forsake you (Hebrews 13:5).

In His name, and for His glory,

Caroline Abbott

Caroline Abbott

APPENDIX - RESOURCES

Phone Numbers/Websites

National Domestic Violence Hotline in the United States 1-800-799-SAFE (7233) or 1-800-787-3224 (TTY) www.thehotline.org

National Domestic Violence Hotline in Canada 1-800-363-9010

National Domestic Violence Hotline in the United Kingdom 0808 2000 247

http://www.hotpeachpages.net Hot Peach Pages—Links to the Domestic Violence agency in every country in the world, in their native language.

http://www.carolineabbott.com, The author's website. Focuses on domestic violence issues from God's perspective.

http://www.troubledwith.com, A website of Focus on the Family—answers questions about the family, relationships, depression, domestic abuse.

Cloud-Townsend Resources, 3176 Pullman Ave, # 104, Costa Mesa, CA 92626, 1-800-676-HOPE (4673) www.cloudtownsend.com.

The State of New Hampshire Governor's Commission on Domestic and Sexual Violence and Attorney General's Office Faith Communities: Domestic Violence Protocol 2007, http://doj.nh.gov/criminal/victim-assistance/documents/faith-communities-protocol.pdf. A protocol created by the state of New Hampshire describing how churches should respond to domestic abuse.

http://cryingoutforjustice.wordpress.com, Pastor Jeff Crippen's website focusing on spiritual abuse in the church.

http://verbalabusejournals.com, Kellie Jo Holly's website focusing on verbal and emotional abuse, and stories of survivors, includes an excellent safety plan.

http://lundybancroft.com, Lundy Bancroft's website. Includes a great list of resources for many types of abused women.

http://cornercanyoncounseling.com, Corner Canyon Counseling and Psychological Services in Utah. Includes information on abuse, trauma, addictions, anger, parenting.

http://www.aedv.org, Advocates to End Domestic Violence in Nevada. Includes Domestic violence facts and myths and safety planning tips.

http://www.bridgesnh.org, Bridges Domestic and Sexual Violence Support in New Hampshire. Includes information on restraining orders, stalking, teen and elder abuse.

http://www.cdv.org, Children of Domestic Violence. Focuses on education and help for children in abusive homes.

http://www.thefamilytree.org, The Family Tree, Colorado. They help with children, homelessness, and domestic violence.

http://www.rbc.net, A Web site of RBC Ministries.

Books

Jay Adams, *Marriage, Divorce, and Remarriage in the Bible* (Grand Rapids, MI:Zondervan, 1980).

George R. Bach and Ronald M. Deutsch, *Stop! You're Driving Me Crazy* (New York:G.P. Putman's Sons, 1980).

Lundy Bancroft, *Why Does He DO That? Inside the Minds of Angry and Controlling Men* (New York, NY:Berkley Books, 2002).

Dr. Henry Cloud and Dr. John Townsend, *Boundaries: When to Say Yes When to Say No to Take Control of Your Life* (Grand Rapids, MI:Zondervan, 1992).

Jeff Crippen and Anna Wood, *A Cry for Justice: How the Evil of Domestic Abuse Hides in Your Church* (United States:Calvary Press Publishing, 2012).

Patricia Evans, *The Verbally Abusive Relationship: How to Recognize It and How to Respond* (Avon, MA:Adams Media Corporation, 1996).

Marie M. Fortune, *Keeping the Faith: Guidance for Christian Women Facing Abuse* (San Francisco:HarperSanFrancisco, 1987).

Patricia Riddle Gaddis, *Battered but Not Broken: Help for Abused Wives and Their Church Families* (Valley Forge, PA:Judson Press, 1996).

Stormie Omartian, *The Power of a Praying Wife* (Eugene, OR:Harvest House Publishers, 1997).

Detective Sgt. Donald Stewart, *Refuge: A Pathway Out of Domestic Violence and Abuse* (Birmingham, AL:New Hope Publishers, 2004).

Other Written Resources

Herb Vander Lugt, "God's Protection of Women: When Abuse is Worse Than Divorce" (Grand Rapids, MI:RBC Ministries, 2005).

J. Allan Petersen, "Your Reactions Are Showing" (Lincoln, NE:Back to the Bible, The Good News Broadcasting Association, Inc, 1967).

ENDNOTES

INTRODUCTION

1. Patricia Evans, *The Verbally Abusive Relationship: How to Recognize It and How to Respond* (Avon, Mass:Adams Media Corporation, 1996), 23.

CHAPTER ONE

2. National Domestic Violence Hotline, "Get Educated—What is Domestic Violence?" http://www.the-hotline.org/geteducated/what-is-domestic-violence?/, accessed December 7, 2012.

3. See the Appendix for Domestic Violence Hotline numbers in other countries besides the United States.

4. Evans, *The Verbally Abusive Relationship,* 24.

5. George R. Bach and Ronald M. Deutsch, *Stop! You're Driving Me Crazy* (New York:G.P. Putman's Sons, 1980), 272-3.

6. For a good description of "gaslighting," see http://www.carolineabbott.com/2012/11/what-is-gaslight-ing-another-word-for-psychological-abuse/

7. A perfect example of psychological abuse from Debbie, once while Debbie's husband was carrying on an affair with their teenaged babysitter, Debbie caught them together at a Wendy's restaurant. When she confronted them, he told her, "You don't see me here, you really must be crazy!"

CHAPTER TWO

8. Advocates to End Domestic Violence, "Domestic Violence Facts—The Cycle of Violence," http://www.aedv.org/index.php/domestic-violence-facts, accessed January 29, 2013.

9. Bridges Domestic and Sexual Violence Support, "What is Domestic Violence," http://www.bridgesnh.org/domestic_violence.php, accessed December 7, 2012. Adapted from Dr. Lenore Walker's "Cycle of Violence."

10. Corner Canyon Counseling and Psychological Services, "Categories of Verbal Abuse," http://corner-canyoncounseling.com, accessed January 29, 2012 (Click on "Education," then "Categories of Emotional Abuse"). Yahoo! Voices, "Types of Verbal Abuse," http://voices.yahoo.com/the-types-verbal-abuse-473142.html?cat=72, accessed January 29, 2013. We Survived Abuse, "Categories of Verbal Abuse," http://jamesfive19.com/blog/?p=700, accessed January 29, 2013.

CHAPTER THREE

11. Lundy Bancroft, *Why Does He DO That? Inside the Minds of Angry and Controlling Men* (New York, NY:Berkley Books, 2002), 23-48.

12. Bancroft, *Why Does He DO That?,* 54-59.

CHAPTER FOUR

13. J. Allan Petersen, *Your Reactions Are Showing* (Lincoln, NE:Back to the Bible, The Good News Broadcast-ing Association, Inc., 1967, reprinted 1996), 5-10. Used by permission.

CHAPTER FIVE

14. John Piper's sermon from June 11, 1989, "Husbands Who Love Like Christ and the Wives Who Submit to Them" http://www.desiringgod.org/resource-library/sermons/husbands-who-love-like-christ-and-the-wives-who-submit-to-them, accessed January 29, 2013.

15. Walter C. Kaiser, Jr., "Correcting Caricatures: The Biblical Teaching on Women," http://walterckaiserjr.com/women.html, accessed January 29, 2013.

CHAPTER SIX

16. Stormie Omartian, *The Power of a Praying Wife* (Eugene, OR:Harvest House Publishers, 1997). For Stormie's discussion of these points, see Chapters 1 and 2, pages 13-46.

17. Stormie Omartian, *The Power of a Praying Wife.* The list of prayer topics runs throughout this book and is part of its organization, thus, I do not cite specific page numbers for each one.

CHAPTER SEVEN

18. Mercy Me, "Here with Me." Simpleville Publishing, LLC. 2004.

CHAPTER EIGHT

19. Robert Anda, Robert Block, Vincent Felitti, Centers for Disease Control and Prevention, Kaiser Permanente's Health Appraisal Clinic in San Diego, "Adverse Childhood Experiences Study—Major Findings." 2003. Available at http://www.cdc.gov/ace/findings.htm, accessed January 29, 2013.

20. See http://www.CDV.org for their video entitled "10 Shocking Domestic Violence Statistics for 2011."

21. CDV.org, "10 Shocking Domestic Violence Statistics."

22. CDV.org, "10 Shocking Domestic Violence Statistics."

23. CDV.org, "10 Shocking Domestic Violence Statistics."

24. Leonard P. Edwards, "Reducing Family Violence: The Role of the Family Violence Council," *Juvenile and Family Court Journal,* (Vol. 1, 1992).

25. Intermedia, Inc., "Hostages at Home: Understanding Domestic Violence" (video) (Seattle, WA).

26. Intermedia, Inc., "Hostages at Home."

27. Intermedia, Inc., "Hostages at Home."

28. Intermedia, Inc., "Hostages at Home."

29. Intermedia, Inc., "Hostages at Home."

30. Intermedia, Inc., "Hostages at Home."

31. Intermedia, Inc., "Hostages at Home."

32. Intermedia, Inc., "Hostages at Home."

33. Laura Crites and Donna Coker, "What Therapists See That Judges May Miss: A Unique Guide to Custody Decisions When Spouse Abuse is Charged," *The Judges Journal,* (Spring 1988), 11.

34. Intermedia, Inc., "Hostages at Home."

35. Murray A. Stauss, Richard J. Gelles, and Christine Smith, *Physical Violence in American Families; Risk Factors and Adaptations to Violence in 8,145 Families* (New Brunswick:Transaction Publishers, 1990).

36. Lundy Bancroft at EADV event, Department of Revenue, Boston, MA on December 15, 2010, *Domestic Violence in Popular Culture,* http://www.youtube.com/watch?v=xuY_mUoplc0 , accessed December 7, 2012.

CHAPTER NINE

37. K. Healey, C. O'Sullivan, & C. Smith, *Batterer Intervention: Program Approaches and Criminal Justice Strategies* (Washington, DC:US Department of Justice, Office of Justice Programs, National Institute of Justice, February 1998).

38. Patricia Riddle Gaddis, *Battered but Not Broken: Help for Abused Wives and Their Church Families* (Valley Forge, PA:Judson Press, 1996) 50.

39. Ibid.

CHAPTER TEN

40. I am indebted to The Family Tree of Wheat Ridge, Colorado for these safety-planning tips for children. Call them at (303) 422-2133, or find them on the Web at http://thefamilytree.org/, accessed February 11, 2012.

CHAPTER FOURTEEN

41. Dr. Henry Cloud and Dr. John Townsend, *Boundaries: When to Say Yes When to Say No to Take Control of Your Life* (Grand Rapids, MI:Zondervan, 1992), 29, 33.

42. Cloud and Townsend, *Boundaries,* 157.

43. Cloud and Townsend, *Boundaries,* 242, 257.

44. Cloud and Townsend, *Boundaries,* 35-36.

CHAPTER FIFTEEN

45. Jay Adams, *Marriage, Divorce, and Remarriage in the Bible* (Grand Rapids, MI:Zondervan, 1980), 11, 16, 17.

46. Dr. Henry Cloud and Dr. John Townsend, *Boundaries: When to Say Yes When to Say No to Take Control of Your Life* (Grand Rapids, MI:Zondervan, 1992), 161-2.

CHAPTER SIXTEEN

47. Patricia Evans, *The Verbally Abusive Relationship: How to Recognize It and How to Respond* (Avon, Mass:Adams Media Corporation, 1996), 117-131.

48. Evans, *The Verbally Abusive Relationship,* 140.

49. Evans, *The Verbally Abusive Relationship,* 140.

CHAPTER SEVENTEEN

50. Detective Sgt. Donald Stewart, *Refuge: A Pathway Out of Domestic Violence and Abuse* (Birmingham, AL:New Hope Publishers, 2004), 230.

CHAPTER NINETEEN

51. Taken from The State of New Hampshire Governor's Commission on Domestic and Sexual Violence and Attorney General's Office Faith Communities: Domestic Violence Protocol 2007, http://doj.nh.gov/criminal/victim-assistance/documents/faith-communities-protocol.pdf, 11.

CHAPTER TWENTY

52. Conversation points for the wife and husband taken from The State of New Hampshire Governor's Commission on Domestic and Sexual Violence and Attorney General's Office Faith Communities: Domestic Violence Protocol 2007, http://doj.nh.gov/criminal/victim-assistance/documents/faith-communities-protocol.pdf, 9-13.

53. Stewart, *Refuge,* 219.

54. K. Healey, C. O'Sullivan, & C. Smith, *Batterer Intervention: Program Approaches and Criminal Justice Strategies* (Washington, DC:US Department of Justice, Office of Justice Programs, National Institute of Justice, February 1998).

55. Stewart, *Refuge*, 216-217.

56. Stewart, *Refuge*, 208-210.

CHAPTER TWENTY-ONE
57. Marie M. Fortune, *Keeping the Faith: Guidance for Christian Women Facing Abuse* (San Francisco:HarperSanFrancisco, 1987), 88.

CHAPTER TWENTY-TWO
58. Taken and adapted from *God's Protection of Women: When Abuse is Worse than Divorce* by Herb Vander Lugt, Copyright 2005 by RBC Ministries, Grand Rapids, MI. Used by permission. All rights reserved.

59. Joe M. Sprinkle, "Old Testament Perspectives on Divorce and Remarriage," *Journal of the Evangelical Theological Society*, December 1997, Vol 40, No. 4, p 3.

60. Dallas Willard, *The Divine Conspiracy*, (New York, NY:HarperCollins, 1997), 171.

61. Herb Vander Lugt, *God's Protection of Women*, 22.

62. Dallas Willard, *The Divine Conspiracy*, 169–170.

63. Herb Vander Lugt, *God's Protection of Women*, 24.

64. Herb Vander Lugt, *God's Protection of Women*, 32.

65. Jeff Crippen and Anna Wood, *A Cry for Justice: How the Evil of Domestic Abuse Hides in Your Church* (United States:Calvary Press Publishing, 2012), 303-305.

66. Crippen, *A Cry for Justice*, 303.

67. Crippen, *A Cry for Justice*, 304.

68. Crippen, *A Cry for Justice*, 293-294.

69. Crippen, *A Cry for Justice*, 294.

70. Crippen, *A Cry for Justice*, 298.

CHAPTER TWENTY-THREE
71. Evans, *The Verbally Abusive Relationship*, 115.

72. Evans, *The Verbally Abusive Relationship*, 114, 115.

CHAPTER TWENTY-FOUR
73. Fortune, *Keeping the Faith*, 27, 33-35, 57-58.

CHAPTER TWENTY-FIVE
74. Gaddis, *Battered but Not Broken*, 37.

CHAPTER TWENTY-SEVEN
75. Gaddis, *Battered but Not Broken*, 9-10.

CHAPTER THIRTY
76. Lundy Bancroft, "Child Custody Justice," http://www.lundybancroft.com/?page_id=134. Also from the book *Disorder in the Courts: Mothers and Their Allies Take on the Family Court System*, an e-book available from California NOW.

CHAPTER THIRTY-TWO

77. Fortune, *Keeping the Faith*, 39.

CHAPTER THIRTY-THREE

78. Vander Lugt, *God's Protection of Women*, 29–30.

79. Vander Lugt, *God's Protection of Women*, 30.

80. Adams, *Marriage, Divorce, and Remarriage in the Bible*, 43–44.

81. Adams, *Marriage, Divorce, and Remarriage in the Bible*, 42.

82. Adams, *Marriage, Divorce, and Remarriage in the Bible*, 42–43.

83. Adams, *Marriage, Divorce, and Remarriage in the Bible*, 85.